a SAVOR THE SOUTH® *cookbook*

Bacon

SAVOR THE SOUTH® *cookbooks*

a SAVOR THE SOUTH® *cookbook*

Bacon

FRED THOMPSON

The University of North Carolina Press CHAPEL HILL

SAVOR THE SOUTH® is a registered trademark of the
University of North Carolina Press, Inc.
Designed by Kimberly Bryant and set in Miller and
Calluna Sans types by Rebecca Evans.

Jacket illustration: © istockphoto.com/milanfoto

Library of Congress Cataloging-in-Publication Data
Names: Thompson, Fred, 1953–
Title: Bacon / Fred Thompson.
Other titles: Savor the South cookbook.
Description: Chapel Hill : The University of
North Carolina Press, [2016] |
Series: A savor the South cookbook | Includes index.
Identifiers: LCCN 2016019961| ISBN 9781469630113
(cloth : alk. paper) | ISBN 9781469630120 (ebook)
Subjects: LCSH: Cooking (Bacon) | Cooking, American—
Southern style. | LCGFT: Cookbooks.
Classification: LCC TX749.5.P67 T46 2016 | DDC 641.6/64—
dc23 LC record available at https://lccn.loc.gov/2016019961

For Karl Knudsen
and the guys at BNO

Contents

a SAVOR THE SOUTH® *cookbook*

Bacon

Introduction

Bacon in the Life of a Southerner

It calls you from a sound sleep. Oh my goodness, what it can do for a pot of peas. We don't think of it as the star, but it is always more than a supporting character. Folks gussie it up in ice cream and chocolate, yet its humble place in the world is always preserved. We have loved it since we were kids. It's been the downfall of many a vegetarian. No cardiologist can take it away, at least not completely. In the South, it sustains us with simple memories and everyday joys from an animal that's easy to raise. Bacon: it seasons our life.

Why? Bacon is "meat candy," that's why. Eating bacon is what we do in the South, and, paraphrasing Rhett Butler, "we don't give a damn" if it's stylish or not. It allows every sense to take part in its pleasure—our ears with its gentle popping as it fries, the fragrance that is always recognizable, the eyes as we ponder the perfect match of fat to lean, and of course our taste, as bacon hits the salty, sweet, textural, and umami receptors of our tongues. Nothing else in the food world can amuse all of the sensory points the way bacon does.

And while it may be all those things, it is also a sustaining food. Bacon reveals to us history, both our own and our beloved South's. Bacon is democratic. Most anyone in our population can afford some kind of bacon. While most of the major meatpacking companies have fiddled with it some, they have been unable to destroy the essential truth in bacon. Even in the face of the mega-industrial food landscape, smaller packers offering artisanal bacons have found their place on the grocers' meat counter.

What Is Bacon?

Bacon is, by definition, a cured and sometimes smoked pork part. Curing pork has a long history, probably dating back to early Chinese dynasties. "Bacon," the noun, is a bit French and German and traditionally refers more to the back of the hog, and the British may have been the first to consider, and cure, a piece of pork called bacon. Bacon is cured with salt, sugar, and other flavorings, either rubbed into the pork using a method called dry packing, or cured wet, in brine. In large operations, the meat may be injected with the brine. The result is fresh bacon, or "green bacon." This bacon can be smoked, fried, grilled, baked, or boiled. Most bacon in America is smoked before being sold to the end consumer. The smoke is what gives bacon its unique appeal, and it is also where bacons differentiate themselves from one another. The smoke can be wafted from smoldering corncobs, hickory, applewood, cherry, or most any other wood.

In America, bacon comes from the belly of the pig. In fact, the U.S. Department of Agriculture defines bacon as "the cured belly of a swine carcass." We seem to like the higher fat-to-lean ratio from the belly. The rest of the world considers this "American-style bacon," or "streaky bacon." People from most other countries tend to prefer their bacon from the meatier, leaner side portions of the hog, such as the loin—this type is often called "back bacon." Canadian and Irish bacon is an example of this style. Italy's pancetta is cured and rolled but never smoked.

More than fifty different styles of bacon happily coexist worldwide. Today's U.S. markets contain many of the world's bacons. As the Latino population has grown in the States, and in the South especially, it has become more common to see jowl or cheek bacon in many markets and other stores that serve a large Latino clientele. This usually is sold under the name *guanciale*. Bacon can also be made from beef, goat, lamb, and especially turkey, and while these preparations conform to many religious or health dietary concerns, this is not bacon and cannot be labeled as such, unless the source of the meat is defined ("beef bacon," for example).

Bacon's Role in the South

Bacon, as a meat that rides low on the hog, belongs to the iconic "three Ms" of traditional southern foodways, as Marcie Cohen Ferris discusses in her book *The Edible South*. Those Ms are meal (wheat flour and cornmeal), meat, and molasses. "These ingredients became crucial, but nutritionally inadequate, foods of the southern working-class table," Marcie comments. As a cheap, filling food, bacon reflects the complexity of southern history and southern cuisine, in which it was an important food for enslaved African Americans in the plantation South and equally important for white folks in the mountain South as well as the fifty-acre farmers and sharecroppers in the region's larger environs. As with a number of foods traditionally eaten by poor people, bacon has now been enthusiastically embraced by many leading figures in the South's contemporary food renaissance. The Southern Foodways Alliance featured a "bacon forest" at one of its recent symposiums, and many southern chefs, male and female, pray at the church of bacon. But bacon will still be a part of the southern culinary fabric long after the bacon silliness is over.

The economics of bacon are clear in our southern heritage. The pig has been a critical piece of the survival puzzle from the earliest days for European settlers who came to call the South home. The first porcine inhabitants of the South were introduced in Florida by Spanish explorer Hernando de Soto in the 1530s. Historian Charles Reagan Wilson, in volume 7 of *The New Encyclopedia of Southern Culture*, tells us that those thirteen pigs started "an enduring hog kingdom that would define the region's cuisine and help to nourish southerners for centuries. By the time English settlers came to Virginia in 1607 with their own domesticated pigs, wild hogs were roaming the countryside."

Domestic hogs were easy to raise in the southern environment. Pork was much easier to cure than the meat from other animals, and it allowed a supply of protein in the months to come. At first hogs were free-roaming and then easily gathered to feed and fatten right before slaughter. This practice worked well for southern farmers; most of them had bottomland, areas that were swampy or otherwise not well suited for crops like cotton and tobacco. My grandfather was a perfect example: he kept his hogs on a low-lying plot in a grove of pine trees. The hogs were happy, and what had been unproductive land now had value. As did the hogs. In the late 1800s, and through the early 1900s, laws were passed that required fencing, which in large part stopped this free-roaming practice.

You know the phrase "eating high on the hog"? It has a real purpose other than describing someone's apparent wealth. For decades, at slaughter, the parts higher on the hog, like the loin, tenderloin, and ribs, had a much higher dollar value than the bellies, shoulders, and hams, and that is somewhat still the case today. My grandfather, and later his sons, would raise three or four hogs a year, and as hog-killing time came around, usually in January, the meat from the first hog killed was divided among the family. But from the next one or two hogs the more salable higher-up parts were sold, and that money was used to start the next year's crops and replace the hogs.

The bellies were cured and smoked for bacon, as were the hams and shoulders, usually by the womenfolk, unless the shoulders became barbecue. Cured hams had a higher market value than raw hams, so many of the cured ones were sold after curing. Fat was rendered for lard, which was used as a cooking medium and, before electricity came into use, as a fuel for lamps. Fatback and the fat with small streaks of lean meat, called "streak o' lean," were salted and placed in a barrel. A full pork barrel was a good thing — and the term moved into our political life to describe how politicians sent funding to their own districts. "Scraping the bottom of the barrel" came when the cured pork was about to run out before the next hog killing.

Raising, killing, and curing hogs was a practice that went back in my family for generations, dating to my ancestors' arrival in this country in the late seventeenth century. They were no different than the thousands of other small-acreage farmers who filled the landscape of the South before and after the Civil War.

Southern foodways were traditionally highly dependent on vegetables and small amounts of protein. Smoked pork, especially bacon, became a main source of meat for the large agricultural population of the South. Bacon fat became a preferred cooking and seasoning ingredient, along with lard and ham trimmings. City dwellers became bacon lovers depending on their knowledge of and distance from local farmers and the farmers' willingness to part with some.

The Great Depression changed the South. Land foreclosure was everywhere, and those who lost their farms gravitated to cities in search of work. They also unwittingly spread the gospel of bacon, which again was embraced as a cheap food source. Many mill villages popped up in the South as industrialization began its march into the South, and most of these villages had "hog lanes" where the residents could set up a hog lot for their family and continue their rural endeavors. After World War II, returning veterans, having seen the world, left the farm in record numbers—they could not see how the family farms they had left for the war could become productive enough to support multigenerational families. My father was one of those vets. Yet from 1946 to his death, his favorite foods remained those he loved from the farm, and bacon, and cooking with bacon fat, was the central character in his food story. Whatever your roots, or wherever you wind up in life, your beloved foods will always follow you in one way or another.

Bacon has had ups and downs as to its "correctness," because there are certain health concerns associated with its consumption. Southerners and all other Americans kept eating it, though—we would just hide it in our grocery carts and not talk about it. Not long ago, high-protein diets came into fashion, so we used that excuse to bring bacon back into our kitchens.

More recently, the "farm to fork" movement has had us searching for bacon from heritage breeds and farm-friendly sources, cured and smoked using the old methods and best practices. This has also been shepherded by the Southern Foodways Alliance, among other forward-thinking groups and folk, in their quest to preserve our southern food values. I think of people like Alan Benton, of Benton's Country Hams in Madisonville, Tennessee, who have embraced our forebears' slow and uncomplicated cures for hams and bacon and have become a national phenomenon, not through slick marketing but through word of mouth. Benton's hams are lauded by award-winning chefs like John Fleer, Sean Brock, David Chang, Ben Barker, Ashley Christiansen, Vivian Howard, and a host of others. His name has become "menu speak" on some of the best restaurants, joints, and dives from coast to coast. Cure masters like Rufus Brown of Johnston County Hams in Smithfield, North Carolina, and Sam Edwards of Edwards Hams in Surry, Virginia, have brought old breeds of hogs back to the forefront in their quest for the finest cured pork products they can offer. (Sadly, Edwards Hams had a devastating fire in its smokehouses. The owners have vowed to rebuild, but it might be two years before they are fully up and running again.) Why are heritage breeds worth saving? Simply put, they are more flavorful and have a better fat-to-lean ratio; they have not gone through breeding practices to enhance growth and leanness in large commercial operations New animal husbandry techniques are being employed to affect flavors and leanness, and a new breed of hog farmer has discovered more humane ways to raise hogs, believing that flavor and quality improve when the hogs are treated with greater respect.

"Bacon (noun): The main reason you are not a vegetarian." I wish I had come up with that little saying. No one person wants to claim it, but the phrase explains a lot. Bacon can and does affect us. It's in our music, novels, and movies. Hillary Scott, a member of the award-winning country music group Lady Antebellum, sums up bacon in the South nicely: "You pretty much can't get away from bacon and whiskey in the South. Put a doughnut in it and you're good to go." Country singer Blake Shelton empowers bacon in his 2008 hit song "Country Strong": "Cat Diesel Power cap pulled down low, making that bacon row by row. Can't get those muscles at the YMCA. It's from chopping cotton . . . and slinging hay. . . . No doubt about it, that boy's country strong." "The Battle of New Orleans," which has been covered by over fifty artists, recalls, "In 1814 we took a little trip along with Colonel Jackson down the mighty Mississip'. We took a little bacon and we took a little beans." In "Behind the Scene," Reba McEntire sings, "I fed the children and kissed them goodnight. You fed the jukebox till they turned out the lights. I bought the bacon and you bought the booze." Just can't get away from bacon and whiskey, can we?

Although the movie *Grumpier Old Men* is not based in the South, it contains one of the great cinematic discussions of bacon.

Burgess Meredith tells Jack Lemmon his secret to a long life: "I get up in the morning and have me a cigarette and five strips of bacon. For lunch I have a bacon sandwich. For an afternoon snack, bacon! I usually drink my supper. Now all those flat bellies keep telling me to change my ways or I'm going to die, but they keep dying and I'm still here." Must be the bacon, don't you think?

Bacon is a character actor in all great southern novels and films, from *The Prince of Tides* to *Steel Magnolias*. You just can't have a movie in the South without bacon, and it seems like there isn't a southern novel without some reference to it. Harper Lee's novel *To Kill a Mockingbird* probably has the best line about bacon ever, in any medium: "There were delicious smells about: Chicken, bacon frying, crisp as twilight air."

Bacon frying, crisp as twilight air.

We are in the age of "baconmania," where everything must be better with bacon, from desserts to soaps to bacon-scented Band-Aids. And that's just fine with me. But bacon, true bacon, will also stand the test of time to a southerner. Smoke, salt, sweet, and grease. Heaven.

Bacon Basics

TYPES OF BACON

As my friend and mentor James Villas, a North Carolina native and award-winning food writer, states in his book on bacon, "Just as real hamburgers are not made with chicken, nor is a martini with vodka, genuine bacon is not made with beef, turkey, or duck." Well put. Bacon in America, and particularly in the South, is traditionally a pork-based product. Yes, you can find and purchase beef- and poultry-based bacon, but in my opinion these products are not, by any stretch of the imagination, bacon. The U.S. Department of Agriculture defines bacon as "the cured belly of a swine carcass"; other cuts and types must be separately qualified (for example, as "smoked pork loin bacon"). The majority of this cookbook deals with pork belly–based bacon products, with the except of Canadian-style bacon, which still is not true bacon but has become a popular lower-fat substitute for traditional bacon and, thanks to its ease of preparation, a favorite of certain fast food chains.

There are three different ways of categorizing bacon. The first is by cure:

* Green bacon is cured but not smoked.
* Uncured bacon is smoked but not cured.
* Most bacon (and the bacon used in most of the following recipes) is both smoked and cured.

Cured bacon is categorized again by the method used in curing.

* Wet-cured bacon is the typical curing process used for large commercial bacon brands, where the bacon is brined in a liquid solution before smoking.
* Dry-cured bacon, my favorite method, where the belly is rubbed with a dry salt and spice mixture to cure before smoking. This is found primarily with homemade bacon and artisanal styles of bacon.
* Nitrate-free bacon is created by using naturally occurring nitrates, especially celery powder, rather than sodium nitrate. (Sounds benign, but a nitrate is still a nitrate, I understand.)

Finally, bacon is categorized according to its cut or style:

* Slab bacon is just what it sounds like: a slab of uncut cured and/or smoked pork belly. The ratio of fat to lean should be, on average, about two-thirds fat to one-third lean. Actually, that is a good ratio to aim for in all American pork belly bacon. This style of bacon will be more readily found in specialty stores.
* Streaky bacon is what the rest of the world calls our typical American style of bacon and what you encounter in most supermarkets. Sliced and vacuumed packed, it usually comes in either of two slice widths. The thin or standard slice, the most common type, is about one-sixteenth of an inch. The thick-cut slice is around one-eighth of an inch

and sometimes, as thick-cut sliced bacon has become all the rage recently, closer to one-quarter of an inch. You might also see thick-cut bacon labeled as "market bacon" when found in the butcher's case, or sometimes "country-style bacon" in an artisanal market. "Center-cut bacon" has about 30 percent less fat than standard-slice bacon and is cut from the section of the belly that was closest to the bone.

✸ Double-smoked bacon is typically slab but sometimes sliced bacon that has spent eighteen to twenty-four hours in the smoker. The flavor is much more intense, and the fat has taken on a golden color. This bacon tends to shrink less when cooking. It is almost always found in specialty or artisanal markets

✸ Pancetta is unsmoked and rolled pork belly dry-cured with salt, spices, and herbs. Used mainly for seasoning, it delivers a distinctly different taste than smoked American bacon. An immigrant from Italy, pancetta is widely used in this country and available in most supermarkets. Much of it is now produced domestically. *Pancetta affumicata* is smoked pancetta that is widely popular in northeastern Italy and is finding its way here through Italian stores and specialty butchers.

✸ Salt pork, or, as southerners call it, streak-o'-lean, is cured, unsmoked, very fatty pork belly with a small amount of lean meat. It is used for seasoning in cooking. I have also heard folks call this white bacon.

Two other styles of bacon are not from the pork belly but are very common and worth mentioning here.

✸ Canadian-style bacon is cured and lightly smoked pork loin, usually just the lean solid eye of the loin, and is most always precooked. Canadians actually call this back bacon. Almost hamlike, it is great for pizza, breakfast sandwiches, and eggs Benedict.

✸ Jowl or cheek bacon is cured and smoked pig cheek. It was a traditional product of the South, but in more recent years, this style of bacon was only found in Italian and Latino markets; in Italy, where it has long been made, it is known as *guanciale*. With the rise of artisanal hog producers, innovative chefs, and specialty butchers, jowl bacon has become more mainstream in the South and beyond. It is more fatty than regular bacon and is mainly used for seasoning.

You can usually find organic bacon in each of the above categories.

BUYING BACON

Learning how to recognize good bacon makes a true bacon connoisseur. It's about color—the color of both the fat and the lean. The fat should look anywhere from white to a no-more-than-pale gold, and the lean should be red to a brown with a distinct red tone. The color indicates how long the bacon has been smoked. Double-smoked bacon breaks this rule: the fat is more of a deep golden, and the lean is much browner but still has a red note.

In any case, the fat should be somewhat firm. Also remember the two-thirds fat to one-third lean ratio when purchasing bacon. If you are buying bacon from a butcher's case, ask the butcher to hold up a piece or two for your inspection. Don't hesitate to burrow into the piles of prepackaged bacon, looking through both the front *and* the back of the package, to get a view from both sides. Many times, what looks meaty from the front is hiding a bunch of fat in the back.

Check the sell date. Also, don't let price be your total guide as to quality. Many expensive bacons are better and worth the extra cost, but some are not, and quite frankly, there is a lot of subpar meat hiding under the "housemade" label. Use these same standards to choose bacon at any price point, and, if possible, know your butcher.

STORING BACON

The standard vacuum-packed and sealed bacon—unopened—generally stays fresh for three to four weeks past its sell date, but once the vacuum is broken, it should be consumed within a week or so in proper refrigeration conditions. Store the bacon in a ziptop plastic bag with as much air removed as possible, and place it in the coldest part of the refrigerator. Slab bacon has a slightly longer life when stored in the same manner. The telltale signs of bacon becoming rancid is a distinct hardening of the fat and a loss of any red tones in the lean meat. Your eyes are your best guide. It takes bacon a long time to smell rancid—a long while past the time when you should eat it.

Salt and fat do not take kindly to freezing. Many folks are dead set against freezing presliced bacon. Most bacon, even presliced, will hold up nicely for a month in the freezer when vacuum-packed or placed in freezer bags with as much air removed as possible. I own a vacuum sealer that I use with my DIY Bacon and have found that homemade bacon can stand up to three or four months in the freezer. If you get into making your own bacon, I would advise you to get a vacuum sealer. Homemade vacuum-sealed bacon can last in the refrigerator for a good month or more. I cut my DIY Bacon into pound slabs, vacuum-seal them, and date them, and it works well.

COOKING BACON

Everybody I know seems to have a secret way to cook bacon. Remember a couple of things before you choose a method. Thin-sliced bacon is designed to be crispy. Thick-cut bacon is really not meant to be crispy, but more chewy and textured. Thin-sliced bacon will also curl and weave more than thick-cut. Liquid-cured bacon will shrivel more than dry-cured. I've cooked more than one hundred pounds of bacon of all cures and thicknesses for this book, and here is my advice by method.

Frying This method is best for regular sliced bacon. Place the bacon in an unheated sauté pan or heavy skillet, such as cast iron. Place the pan over low heat and cook, turning once, until it reaches the desired crispness—about eight minutes for chewy bacon, fifteen for crispy. Remove the bacon to a paper-towel-lined plate and reserve the fat in a heatproof container. An old, clean coffee can works well, though you can also buy a ceramic bacon fat jar. Bacon fat is a wonderful thing, and I'll talk about it later. Do *not* add any other fat to the bacon drippings in this vessel.

Broiling For cooking large amounts of bacon, broiling is certainly convenient. Preheat the broiler and lay slices of bacon over a slotted broiling rack. Broil about 4 inches from the heat for 6–11 minutes, depending on the crispness desired. Turn the bacon once, and keep a close eye on it to prevent burning. Those last few minutes go pretty fast. Remove the bacon to a paper-towel-lined plate, and reserve the bacon fat in your container.

Baking This is my favorite method for cooking bacon and the absolute best method for cooking thick-cut and dry-cured bacons. The method is simple but not my own. The morning cooks at the Durham, North Carolina, Whole Foods Market, where Duke University students eat bacon by the piled plateful, cook the best bacon I've ever eaten. The method? Preheat the oven to 375°. Cover a rimmed baking sheet with parchment paper. Lay the bacon slices out on the paper and bake for 25–30 minutes depending on how done you want it. Remove the sheet from the oven and place a saucier-type pan under one end, allowing the fat to drain to one end of the pan. After a few minutes, transfer the bacon to a platter lined with paper towels. Reserve the fat in your container. My suggestion for any bacon that you don't eat at that moment is to place it in a food storage bag and refrigerate. You now have your own precooked bacon that you can reheat that is a hundred times better than *any* precooked bacon on the market today, and it's about a third of the price.

Microwaving Cooking bacon in the microwave works better with a microwave rack. One advantage to using a rack is that it allows you to collect the bacon fat for other uses. Place the bacon on the rack and cover with paper towels. Cook, on high, for about 1–1½ minutes per slice. Without a rack, place the bacon on a paper-towel-lined plate and then cover with paper towels, Cook as directed above. I'm not a big fan of the microwave, but I know it has become like a second set of hands in some households. I do use the microwave for reheating baked bacon from the above section. Place the baked bacon on a paper-towel-lined plate and cover with paper towels. Cook on high for 10–20 seconds.

Blanching Sometimes you need to blanch bacon. This is true if you are wrapping another item in bacon and you want to make sure that the bacon gets crisp without overcooking the item you have wrapped. Diced bacon (*lardons*) need blanching and then crisping until brown (about 8 minutes). Salt pork should usually be blanched to render some salt. The process is the same for each. Place the bacon in a deep skillet or saucepan and cover with water. Place over high heat and bring to a boil. Reduce the heat to a low simmer and cook for about 3 minutes. Drain and place the bacon on paper towels to finish draining the water.

News Flash: Cooking Bacon in Water This is a new method of cooking bacon that I personally think washes out some of the bacon's flavor. Place the bacon in a skillet and almost cover with water. Place over medium heat and cook until the water has evaporated, then increase the heat and cook till brown and crisp. This method supposedly gives you a more tender bacon without the fear of burning the bacon. Okay, if you want to try it, feel free.

A Word about Health, Nitrates, and Nitrites

I believe we have gotten over our fat phobia of the 1980s, because since then we have learned that sugars and unrefined white flour (pasta, bread) in great quantities may play a bigger role in causing health problems. Still, putting bacon on everything we eat would be just as short-sighted. Bacon is a sensual joy to be savored, not something that we can eat with such abandon that we forget we are eating it. While bacon is free of trans fats and has some good stuff like proteins, potassium, and zinc, it is still high in fat, cholesterol, and sodium. Most bacon is made with nitrates and nitrites, which may be carcinogens. These additives are there for color, flavor, and, most of all, preservation. I have no dog in this fight, although I have health conditions that give me pause regarding fat and sodium.

The U.S. Department of Agriculture heavily controls the use of these additives, trying to ensure safe levels. Commercial nitrate- and nitrite-free products use naturally occurring nitrates and nitrites like those found in celery. In the DIY Bacon section of this book, I do include a curing salt that includes nitrites. I feel that it is safer to use it, at least while you go through the process of curing bacon a few times. I have also cured the bacon without the curing salt. The finished product is less red and does not stay fresh as long. If you are concerned about sodium, there are excellent products on the market that have less of it, and you can also greatly reduce the amount of fat by using the leaner center-cut bacons. I think Julia Child, who lived into her nineties, said it best: "Eat all things in moderation." I would add, "And take the time to enjoy what you eat."

That Wonderful Stuff Called Bacon Fat

Bacon fat, or drippings if you prefer, is one of the great wonders of the culinary world. I know, I know—you expect me to make that comment because I'm a southerner. But think about this historically for a moment. Long before we knew how to convert vegetables to oil or had ever heard about canola or olive oil, every region of our country used meat fats to cook with. Nothing from a slaughtered animal could be wasted. In the South, hogs were the animal of choice because they were inexpensive to raise and required relatively little land. Rendered pork fat—lard—became *the* cooking medium. Straight-up bacon fat, with its salty-sweet cure and smoke, became a treasured flavoring ingredient. I often tell my cooking classes that there are two things that can fix a lackluster dish, and they are from opposite ends of the price spectrum: bacon fat and truffle oil.

Store bacon fat in an airtight heatproof container. The old-fashioned way is a clean coffee can, but many of us no longer buy coffee that way, so a wide-mouth Mason jar is a good substitute. The fat can stay at room temperature for about a month, though organic, nitrate-free bacon fat will last only about two to three weeks before developing a rancid, off-putting smell. The bacon fat should smell like freshly cooked bacon. If it turns rancid, discard it, clean the jar, and start fresh again.

If you plan to store the fat for more than a month, you should clarify it. No, my grandmother or mother never clarified bacon fat, but they used more of it, and they used it more quickly than most of us today will. It's simple to do—just follow the recipe on page 18. Clarifying the fat removes any impurities and tiny bits of bacon that will cause the fat to go rancid. It also creates a better product for making bacon mayonnaise (to die for) and using bacon fat in a piecrust (you need to try that as well). Clarified bacon fat will last for a long time in the refrigerator.

Bacon fat can give foods a depth of flavor that is almost mystical. Earthy and comforting, the fragrance alone of something cooking in bacon fat is intoxicating. A little goes a long way, however. I routinely combine bacon fat with a neutral fat when cooking, something on the line of 1 part bacon fat to 2 parts other fat (like canola oil). Sautéing some onions in this mix will drive you crazy. Use bacon fat with soups, stews, apples, and of course greens and other vegetables. I like to add a tablespoon of bacon fat to the oil that I'm frying chicken in. That's also good when frying fish and shrimp. You mimic the flavor of frying in lard a bit, giving you that old-time flavor you remember from your grandmother's kitchen. But please remember—use small amounts. You want the essence of the bacon, not a cooking fat that totally covers up the flavor of what you are cooking.

Bacon Fat Mayonnaise

This stuff is just plain good. Use it in place of regular mayonnaise anywhere. It definitely pops the flavor on a BLT or burger.

MAKES ABOUT ½ PINT

1 pasteurized egg yolk
¾ teaspoon Dijon mustard
1 teaspoon fresh lemon juice
Sea salt and freshly ground black pepper
½ cup bacon fat, liquid but not hot

Add the egg yolk, mustard, and lemon juice in the small bowl of a food processor or blender. Process to mix. Add some salt and pepper.

With the machine running, add the bacon fat slowly until the mixture begins to stiffen and becomes mayonnaise-like, about 2 minutes. At this point you can add the fat more quickly. If the mayonnaise becomes too thick, add a little boiling water to thin it. Taste and reseason, then reserve. Keeps refrigerated for about 4 days.

Clarified Bacon Fat

I learned this very simple method for clarifying bacon fat in culinary school.

MAKES ABOUT 1 CUP

1 cup rendered bacon fat
2 cups cold water, divided

Place the bacon fat in a small saucepan. Add 1 cup of water and bring to a boil over high heat. Reduce heat to medium and boil for 2 minutes. Transfer this mixture to a heat-proof container—a large Mason jar is perfect for this—and add the remaining water. Refrigerate for about 6 hours or until the fat has solidified. The mixture will have separated into a layer of clarified fat and a layer of water. Remove the solidified fat and discard the water. Place the fat in an airtight container and store in the refrigerator for 4 weeks or freeze up to 6 months.

Bacon Fat Piecrust

This piecrust is killer with an apple pie recipe.

MAKES 2 (9-INCH) PIECRUSTS

3 cups all-purpose flour
¾ teaspoon kosher salt
1½ sticks unsalted butter, chilled and cubed
4 tablespoons clarified bacon fat
1 teaspoon vodka or apple cider vinegar
3–5 tablespoons ice-cold water

In a large bowl or food processor, blend the flour and salt together. Add the butter and bacon fat and blend until the mixture looks like coarse meal and the pieces of fat are about the size of BBs. Stir in the vodka or vinegar.

Add the ice water, 1 tablespoon at a time, until the dough comes together and begins to hold its shape without being crumbly. Form the dough into 2 discs and cover with plastic wrap. Refrigerate for 30 minutes. (The dough will keep up to 3 days refrigerated or 1 month frozen.)

Use as needed for any pie recipe.

DIY Bacon

Yes, it really is easier than you think to make bacon at home, and once you have experienced the craft and the true flavor of bacon made at home, you will be the envy of all your bacon-eating coterie.

DIY Basic Bacon

Making your own bacon at home is simpler than you might think. Finding a fresh pork belly used to be difficult, but now most specialty shops and stores like Whole Foods Market carry them or can order them for you. Also check with your pork producers at the local farmers' market. You can really custom-tailor your bacon to your likes with savory, sweet, and heat. Use these recipes as a starting point and then have some fun. Just keep the salt ratios intact.

I thank Michael Ruhlman at least once a week for his wonderful book Charcuterie, *which has taken this European tradition and introduced it to American cookery. Had it not been for Michael, I would never have started making my own bacon. But I'm here to tell you that once you've done it, you will be hard pressed to ever pick up another pound of processed store-bought bacon again. There really is that much difference. I encourage you to try this recipe. I think you'll become a convert like me—great bacon is best made at home.*

1 (5- to 6-pound) slab fresh pork belly (order this from a
   specialty market, butcher shop, or the pork guy at the
   farmers' market)
¼ cup firmly packed light brown sugar
¼ cup coarsely ground black pepper
¼ cup (2 ounces) kosher salt (I prefer Morton for this)
2 teaspoons pink curing salt #1 (available at spice shops,
   online, and where canning items are sold)
2 tablespoons dried juniper berries, lightly crushed with the
   edge of a heavy skillet
1 teaspoon freshly grated nutmeg
10 garlic cloves, smashed with the flat side of a knife
10 sprigs fresh thyme
4 bay leaves, crumbled
Recommended wood: Hickory, apple, or cherry

Place the pork belly on a cutting board and trim the edges to
square it up nicely. Throw any pieces that you've cut off into a
freezer bag and freeze for another use.

In a small bowl, combine the brown sugar, pepper, salts,
juniper berries, nutmeg, garlic, thyme, and bay leaves. Rub this
mixture on all sides of the belly. Place it in a 2½-gallon ziptop
plastic bag. Pour any remaining spice mixture into the bag and
give it all one last rub. Seal the bag, forcing out as much air as
possible. Place the belly flat on a shelf in the refrigerator for
4 days.

Open the bag and rub the spices back into the pork. Close the
bag, again, forcing out as much air as possible, and refrigerate
for 3 days.

Press on the pork belly—it should be somewhat firm, but not
solid; to be ready for smoking, it should still give but be much

SALT CALCULATION

If your pork belly is short of 5 pounds or more than 5 pounds, use this formula suggested by Michael Ruhlman in his cookbook, *Charcuterie: The Craft of Salting, Smoking, and Curing* to calculate the amount of salt you need for the cure. Multiply the weight of the belly in ounces (there are 16 ounces in a pound) by .025: that's how much salt you should use. Many times after I trim a piece of pork belly, I wind up coming closer to 4 pounds than to 5, so I'll do the math for you. That's 1.6 ounces of kosher salt for about 4 pounds, and ¼ cup kosher salt is 2 ounces. If you don't have a scale, find a neighbor who does. Guesstimating invariably leads to oversalting.

firmer than it was at the start of this process. If it's still a little mushy, put it back in the refrigerator for another couple of days.

Remove the belly from the bag and completely rinse off all of the cure under cold running water. Pat the belly completely dry. Some suggest placing the belly, unwrapped, back in the refrigerator to dry out and develop what's called a pellicle, a tacky surface that allows a meat to absorb more smoke. For making bacon, I find this step unnecessary.

Light a fire in the smoker. Set the temperature for 200–250°. Add the belly and wood chunks. Smoke the belly for 1½–2 hours, until the internal temperature is 150° F. Guess what? You now have bacon. Let the bacon cool a bit and then go ahead and slice off a piece and cook it in a heavy skillet over low heat, turning often. The bacon will keep up to 2 weeks in the refrigerator and 3 months in the freezer.

Maple-Infused Bacon

If you want the maple flavor to be pronounced, you should slow-roast the belly in the oven. Of course you could smoke this one if you like, as above, but I've found that if you smoke it, the maple flavor gets a little lost in the smoke.

MAKES ABOUT 5 POUNDS

1 (5-pound) pork belly, skin on
¼ cup kosher salt (I prefer Morton's)
2 teaspoons pink curing salt #1 (available at spice shops,
    online, and where canning items are sold)
¼ cup maple sugar
1 tablespoon firmly packed dark brown sugar
½ cup Grade B maple syrup

Mix the cure ingredients and rub into the belly. Then proceed as in DIY Basic Bacon to cure.

Preheat the oven to 200°. Place the cured belly on a rack set over a rimmed baking sheet.

Bake the belly for 1½–2 hours or until the internal temperature is 150°. You now have bacon!

Spicy Chili Bacon

Want some kick to your bacon? Here's the answer. Spicy and smoky, it will wake you up in the morning and perk up a BLT at lunch.

MAKES ABOUT 5 POUNDS

---

1 (5-pound) pork belly, skin on
¼ cup (2 ounces) kosher salt (I prefer Morton's)
2 teaspoons pink curing salt #1 (available at spice shops, online, and where canning items are sold)
¼ cup Sriracha sauce
1 tablespoon chipotle hot sauce
1 tablespoon habanero hot sauce

Mix the cure ingredients together and rub into the belly. Then proceed as in DIY Basic Bacon.

Homemade Canadian Bacon

Canadian bacon is another of those products that is so much better when you make it at home. This style of bacon is actually a smoked, cured pork loin; a wet brine is used for the cure. It's simple and will do wonders for your breakfast sandwich. Also try it as a topping for pizza or burgers.

MAKES ABOUT 3½ POUNDS

1 gallon water
1¼ cups kosher salt (I prefer Morton's)
½ cup sugar
½ cup firmly packed light brown sugar
8 teaspoons pink curing salt #1 (available at spice stores, online, or where canning items are sold)
1 tablespoon dried juniper berries, lightly crushed
8 sprigs fresh thyme
8 sprigs fresh sage
4 garlic cloves, smashed with the flat side of a knife
1 (4-pound) boneless pork loin
Recommended wood: Apple

Combine all the ingredients except the pork in a pot and bring to a simmer over medium heat, stirring to dissolve the salt and sugars. Remove from the heat, let cool to room temperature, and refrigerate until cold.

Remove all the fat and silverskin from the pork loin. Place it in a container large enough to hold the loin and brine. Pour the brine over and put a plate or other weighted object on top to hold the pork completely submerged in the brine. Refrigerate for 48 hours.

Remove the loin and discard the brine. Rinse the loin under cold running water and pat dry. Place on a rack set over a tray or sheet pan and refrigerate, uncovered, for 24 hours. This allows the loin to dry, creating a tacky surface called the pellicle, which enables the smoke to penetrate the loin more fully.

Light a fire in the smoker. Set the temperature for 200–250°. Add the wood chunks and the meat, then smoke to an internal temperature of 150° F, usually around 2 hours but possibly as many as 3. Let cool completely, then cover and refrigerate for up to 2 weeks or freeze for up to 3 months.

Home-Cured Pancetta

While pancetta is of Italian heritage, it is quickly becoming a highly prized ingredient in America. There is a ton of domestically produced pancetta on the market today, and it's perfect when you want an herbaceous hammieness without the smoke. You really don't need to dry the pancetta, but your product will have better, more intense flavor, and will last longer if you do. This recipe is again a nod to cookbook author Michael Ruhlman, who wrote Charcuterie, *but I like a more intensely flavored pancetta and have come up with a cure that I, and those who have had it, really enjoy.*

MAKES ABOUT 4½ POUNDS

---

1 (5-pound) slab pork belly, skin removed
4 garlic cloves, minced
2 teaspoons pink salt
¼ cup (2 ounces) kosher salt
2 tablespoons firmly packed dark brown sugar
2 tablespoons juniper berries, crushed slightly
4 bay leaves, crumbled
1 teaspoon freshly grated nutmeg
4 or 5 sprigs fresh thyme
4 (6-inch-long) sprigs of rosemary
5 tablespoons cracked black peppercorns, divided

Trim the pork belly so that its edges are neat and square. Combine the garlic, pink salt, kosher salt, brown sugar, juniper berries, bay leaves, nutmeg, thyme, rosemary, and half the pepper in a bowl and mix thoroughly.

Rub the mixture all over the pork belly. Place the belly in a 2-gallon ziptop plastic bag or in a covered nonreactive container just large enough to hold it. Refrigerate for 7 days. Without removing the pork belly from the bag, rub the pork belly to redistribute the seasonings and flip it over every other day.

After 7 days, check the pork belly for firmness. If it feels firm at its thickest point, it's cured. If it still feels fleshy, refrigerate it with the cure for 1 to 2 more days.

Remove the pork belly from the bag or container, rinse the cure off under cold water, and pat it dry. Sprinkle the meat side of the belly with the remaining pepper.

Starting from a long side, roll up the pork belly tightly, and tie it very tightly with butcher's string at 1- to 2-inch intervals. It's important that there are no air pockets. Using the string to suspend it, hang the rolled pancetta in a cool, humid place to dry for 2 weeks, away from direct sunlight. I hang mine in my laundry room. The pancetta should be firm but pliable, not hard. If you feel the pancetta is getting hard, then wrap it in plastic wrap and refrigerate. After drying, the pancetta can be wrapped in plastic and refrigerated for 3 weeks or more, or frozen for up to 4 months. I slice mine into chunks and vacuum seal them.

CURING SALTS: THE SCOOP

Pink salt, a curing salt with nitrite, is called by different names and sold under various brand names, such as T.C.M., DQ Curing Salt, and Insta Cure #1. The nitrite in curing salts does some unique things to meat. It changes and enhances the flavor, preserves the meat's red color, prevents fats from developing rancid flavors, and prevents many bacteria from growing.

Party-Worthy Bacon

Bacon has never met a party or gathering it didn't like. Bacon really came into fashion as a party food in the 1950s. Some of the recipes in this chapter are throwbacks to those classics, with plenty of current takes on party bacon to keep everybody interested and their taste buds happy.

Devils on Horseback

This is a total throwback to the 1950s. What? You think we only discovered bacon in this decade? This must-have retro party food is making a resurgence on the cocktail buffets of today. And why not? You get sweet, salty, smoky, and earthy, all in one bite. And they're really simple to make.

SERVES 8

8 slices hickory-smoked bacon, each slice cut into thirds
24 pitted dried plums (sometimes referred to as prunes)

Preheat the oven to 400°.

Line a large rimmed baking sheet with foil or parchment.

Wrap a bacon third around each prune and secure with a toothpick. Continue until all the prunes have been wrapped. Place them on the baking sheet and bake until the bacon is browned, usually about 15–20 minutes. Flip the devils halfway through the baking time. Serve straight from the oven.

Slow Cooker Bacon Jam

This is probably the ultimate in bacon cookery. It's a wonderful savory spread for almost anything and a welcome holiday appetizer. Bacon jam goes much further than just what the word implies. When spread over pizza dough, it elevates pizza to another level. One of the best uses for bacon jam—that is, if you can part with it—is to fill 4-ounce canning jars with the stuff and give as gifts. It's so versatile that you'll never run out of uses for it. The beauty of this recipe is that thanks to slow cooker you're not stuck stirring and stirring and stirring until the jam is thickened.

MAKES AT LEAST 3 CUPS

1½ pounds thick-cut applewood- or cherrywood-smoked bacon

2 medium yellow onions, peeled and finely diced

4 garlic cloves, peeled and smashed with the back of a knife

½ cup apple cider vinegar

½ cup firmly packed dark brown sugar

¼ cup pure Grade B maple syrup

¾ cup brewed dark-roast coffee

Slice the bacon into roughly 1-inch pieces.

Put the bacon slices in a large (at least 12-inch) skillet or sauté pan. Place the pan over medium heat and cook until the fat is rendered and the bacon is lightly browned, about 25–30 minutes. Stir the bacon occasionally.

Remove the bacon from the pan using a slotted spoon and place it in the slow cooker's container. Drain off all but about 2 tablespoons of the bacon fat from the pan. Place the pan back over the heat and add the onions. Cook the onions until they are lazy and translucent, about 6 minutes. Add the garlic and continue cooking for another minute or 2, until it is fragrant. Add the vinegar, brown sugar, syrup, and coffee. Increase the heat to high and bring the mixture to a boil, scraping any brown bits from the skillet. This process should take about 2 minutes. Pour the liquid into the slow cooker.

Set the slow cooker for high and cook uncovered until the liquid is syrupy, usually about 3½–4 hours. Transfer this mixture to a food processor and pulse until coarsely chopped. Remove to an airtight container and let cool. Refrigerate for up to 4 weeks.

Caramelized Onion and Bacon Dip

Your friends and family will long remember how the sweetness of the onions combines with the ethereal flavors of bacon. There is nothing that you can buy from your dairy case that can touch this recipe passed on to me from my friend Nikki Parrish of Richmond, Virginia.

MAKES 4 CUPS

8 strips smoked bacon
2 tablespoons unsalted butter
1 medium yellow onion, chopped
1 medium red onion, chopped
1 tablespoon firmly packed light brown sugar
1 tablespoon red wine vinegar
1 cup sour cream (low-fat works)
8 ounces cream cheese, softened (low-fat works)
2 cups shredded Monterey Jack cheese
¼ cup diced green onion
Tortilla chips or crudité for serving

Cook the bacon in a large skillet over medium-low heat until crisp, about 10–15 minutes. Remove the bacon to a paper-towel-lined plate, let cool, then crumble. Remove all but about 2 tablespoons of bacon fat from the skillet.

Add the butter to the skillet with the bacon fat. When the butter starts to foam, stir in the yellow and red onion. Sprinkle the brown sugar over the onions and cook over medium heat until soft and caramelized, about 15 minutes, stirring frequently.

Add the vinegar and crumbled bacon to the onions and remove from the heat. Stir in the sour cream and cream cheese. Blend in 1½ cups of the Monterey Jack cheese.

Preheat the oven to 350°.

Lightly grease a 1-quart baking dish. Pour the mixture into the baking dish and sprinkle the remaining cheese over the top.

Bake for 15–20 minutes or until the cheese is bubbly around the edges. Sprinkle with green onions and serve with tortilla chips or crudité.

Pig Candy

Pig candy is nothing more than bacon cooked with a coating of brown sugar and, for me, crushed red pepper. It's wickedly simple yet incredibly delicious. The beginnings of pig candy are vague, but general consensus has it starting on the cocktail party circuit in Washington, DC. Since nothing really ever gets started in Washington, I suspect that pig candy was an import from some southern hostess. Lou's on Vine, a small, dimly lit wine bar in Hollywood, is famous for serving pig candy as bar food. It has achieved underground cult status in major metropolitan areas from California to New York.

My first sampling of this lacquered loveliness was in Mendocino, California, at a place called the Brewery Gulch Inn. The chef there served what I now call pig candy as the standard bacon with breakfast. He told me that he just wanted to jazz things up. I have since discovered that his roots are in the South. Some of the best pig candy that I've sampled was at a Southern Foodways Alliance event in the heart of the Mississippi Delta.

Years ago I started a ritual of a Christmas Eve party and included pig candy as part of the offerings. Maybe it was the special cocktail that was being consumed at a rapid pace, but the pig candy went flying into people's mouths. "Oh my God, what is this!" was the general reaction. "Can I have the recipe?" I shuffled my feet with false modesty and replied, "It's nothing but bacon and brown sugar, it's really easy to make"—but no recipe was forthcoming. In my neighborhood, if you give up a recipe too easily—well, let's just say you don't. Last year my backdoor neighbor, Linda Johnson, was insistent on helping me prepare for the party. What I really needed was someone to polish the silver. That's sort of tacky to ask, but of course she said yes, and she followed up with, "Aren't your ovens going to be busy? Can I cook something?" I replied, much to her delight, "If you polish my silver, I'll let you make the pig candy." She polished my silver and baked the pig candy this year too. Shades of Tom Sawyer.

16 slices (about 1 pound) bacon, the best quality you can find
1½ teaspoons crushed red pepper, or more if you like
⅓ cup firmly packed light brown sugar, or more if you like

Preheat the oven to 350°. Line two 10 × 15-inch rimmed baking sheets with parchment paper and place a wire rack on top of each sheet (if you skip this step, you will be cleaning the pans into the next decade). Arrange the bacon in a single layer on the two racks. Sprinkle evenly with the pepper and brown sugar.

Bake until the bacon is crisp and browned, rotating the sheet pans in the oven halfway through the process. Some people turn the bacon, but I don't; it's too much trouble for too little result. Move it from the racks onto a plate and pat lightly with a paper towel to remove any remaining grease. Serve hot or at room temperature. You can make this several hours in advance, and keep at room temperature. I have never tried making it a day ahead.

Bacon-Baked Oysters à la Chick's

This is a down-home version of Oysters Rockefeller. It's my adaptation of the oysters served at Chick's restaurant on the Chesapeake Bay side of Virginia Beach. Let's see how many southern ingredients we can get in this. Pimento cheese?—check. Collard greens?—check. And, of course, bacon.

SERVES 6–8

36 oysters on the half shell
¾ cup pimento cheese
2¼ cup cooked collard greens
9 slices bacon, cut in quarters crosswise
Unseasoned breadcrumbs for sprinkling

Preheat the oven to 350°.

Line two rimmed baking sheets with aluminum foil. Divide the oysters between the two baking sheets. Top each oyster with 1 teaspoon of pimento cheese, 1 tablespoon of the collard greens, and 1 piece of bacon, and then dust with the breadcrumbs. Place the pans in the oven and bake for about 10 minutes or until the bacon is slightly browned.

NOTE ❋ Chick's also throws on some sliced jalapeños. Feel free to follow suit if you so desire.

Grilled Bacon Jalapeño Poppers

Stuffed jalapeños are the rage for summer parties—and with good reason, given that this simple recipe is extremely tasty. Play with the cheese mixture any way you like, and look at this as a starting point for customizing this recipe for you and your family.

SERVES 6

**6 fresh large jalapeño peppers, cut in half lengthwise
(seeded or not; if you want more heat, leave the seeds in)
8 ounces cream cheese (low-fat works)
12 slices center-cut bacon**

Build a charcoal fire or preheat the gas grill for high heat.

Fill each jalapeño half with cream cheese, wrap snugly with a slice of bacon, and secure with a toothpick.

Place on the preheated grill, cream cheese side up, and cook until the bacon is crispy and nicely browned, usually about 8 minutes. Serve immediately.

A Little
Breakfast Magic

Most of us grew up with bacon being a breakfast meat. What a way to start the morning—with the smell of bacon wafting through our half-awake brains! There is nothing better than a simple rasher of bacon alongside perfectly cooked eggs and a mound of butter-laden grits. However, bacon can play a starring role in all manner of morning goodness. From breakfast sandwiches to coffee cakes with bacon, this chapter will awaken bacon's day-starting potential.

Bacon Cheddar Grits

While I've put this recipe in the breakfast chapter, these grits are also wonderful under a grilled pork chop or braised short ribs, or alongside fried chicken. I'm confident you'll find many uses for this recipe.

SERVES 4

4 slices thick-cut bacon, finely chopped
4½ cups water
1 cup quick-cooking grits
Kosher salt and freshly ground pepper, to taste
1½ cups shredded sharp cheddar cheese, divided

Place a 3-quart saucepan over medium heat and throw in the bacon. Cook slowly, rendering out the fat and stirring occasionally until the bacon bits are browned, about 8–10 minutes. Remove the bacon with a slotted spoon and place on a paper-towel-lined plate. Reserve.

Remove the saucepan from the heat and carefully add the water. The bacon drippings left in the pan are going to pop and sputter, so take care.

Place the pan back over the heat and bring to a boil over high heat. Vigorously whisk in the grits and continue to whisk until the grits have thickened slightly. Reduce heat to low and keep at a simmer for about 25 minutes, stirring occasionally to prevent the grits from sticking. Season with the salt and pepper and stir in 1 cup of the cheese and the reserved bacon. Simmer for another couple of minutes or until the cheese is melted into the grits.

Pour into a serving dish. Top with the remaining cheese and serve immediately.

NOTE ❉ If at any time the grits become too thick, just add some more water to the pan.

Spinach and Bacon Frittata

My Portuguese friend and assistant Joseph Teresa introduced me to frittatas, and I'm glad he did. It's an interesting play on eggs and a simple way to feed a crowd at breakfast. The ingredients can vary based on what's in season or what you have on hand. A frittata is more impressive to guests than a big skillet full of scrambled eggs, and a whole lot easier for the cook than omelets or fried eggs. Give this a try; I think you will find that it's a nice time saver.

SERVES 4

---

6 large farm-fresh eggs

1 cup ricotta cheese, whole or 2%

1/4 cup grated Gruyère

Kosher salt and freshly ground black pepper

6 strips applewood-smoked bacon, coarsely chopped

5 boiled potatoes, quartered (confession: I have been known
    to use canned or frozen potatoes when time is short)

1 (16-ounce) bag cleaned baby spinach, roughly chopped

Preheat the oven to 350°.

In a medium bowl whisk together the eggs, ricotta, Gruyère, about ½ teaspoon of salt, and several grindings of pepper.

Add the bacon to a 10-inch nonstick oven-proof skillet or sauté pan and cook it over medium heat until crisp and browned, about 8–10 minutes. Pour all but about 1 teaspoon of fat into your bacon drippings jar. Return the pan to the stove and add the potatoes, cooking until warmed through, about 4 minutes. Throw in the spinach and toss until just barely wilted, about 30–60 seconds.

Pour the egg mixture into the pan and stir until slightly thickened, about a minute or two. Transfer the pan to the oven and bake until the center is about set, usually about 15 minutes, but sometimes as much as 20 minutes.

To serve, run a spatula around the edge of the frittata and slide it onto a serving plate. Slice and serve.

Bacon Sour Cream Coffee Cake
with Maple Glaze

I am not a baker: there is measuring involved. I am more the type to add a dash and splash, roast and boast; I am a meat-and-heat kind of guy. That is why, when it comes to baking, I call on Belinda Ellis, editor of Edible Piedmont *magazine. She actually likes to bake and always has, with all the southern mama and apron-strings stories that bakers love. Perhaps bakers just like to eat breads and cake, which she does. Let them bake, and I (and now you) will enjoy the results. This bacon topping is really damn good.*

MAKES 12 SERVINGS

FOR THE CAKE
1½ cups all-purpose flour
⅔ cup firmly packed brown sugar
1 teaspoon ground cinnamon
6 tablespoons unsalted butter, softened
½ teaspoon baking soda
¼ cup maple syrup
½ cup sour cream, whole (not skim or low-fat)
1 egg yolk
1 teaspoon vanilla or maple extract
¾ cup chopped pecans
10 slices chopped cooked bacon

FOR THE GLAZE
½ cup powdered sugar
2 tablespoons maple syrup

Preheat the oven to 350°. Coat an 8-inch square pan with butter. To make the cake, combine the flour, brown sugar, cinnamon, and butter in a mixing bowl or food processor. Mix until combined. Reserve ½ cup of the mixture. Set aside. Add baking soda, maple syrup, sour cream, egg yolk, and extract. Stir to combine. (The mixture will be lumpy.) Spread the batter in the prepared pan.

If you want, use a food processor to chop the pecans and bacon. Combine with the reserved mixture. Sprinkle over the cake. Bake for 25 to 30 minutes or until a toothpick inserted is clean when removed.

To make the glaze, combine the powdered sugar and maple syrup. Drizzle over the cake. Serve warm.

Bacon Apple Pancake

To be honest with you, I don't like mornings. Breakfast for me is more of a weekend event. This bacon-filled apple pancake makes me look forward to those Saturdays and Sundays, especially during the winter, when there are no chores to hurry into.

MAKES ABOUT 5 PANCAKES

---

10 slices bacon
1¼ cup self-rising soft wheat flour such as White Lily,
     Southern Biscuit, or Our Best
1 tablespoon sugar
¾ cup whole milk
1 large egg, lightly beaten
1 tart apple such as Winesap, grated

Preheat the oven to 350°. Place the bacon on a baking sheet and bake for 25 minutes or until it is cooked and crisp. Let it cool completely, reserve all of the drippings. Break the bacon into ½- to 1-inch chunks.

In a medium bowl, combine the flour and sugar. In another bowl, combine the milk, egg, and apple. Pour the milk mixture into the flour and stir just until combined.

Heat a griddle or skillet over medium-high heat. Add 1 teaspoon or so of the reserved bacon drippings. Pour about ⅓ cup of the batter onto the pan. Sprinkle the bacon over the raw batter to cover in a single layer. Cook until bubbles appear in the batter, about 2 minutes. Turn and cook until done, about a minute more. Serve immediately or place in a 200° oven to keep warm.

Bacon and Cheddar Biscuits

Biscuits are a mainstay of a southern breakfast. In Biscuits: A Savor the South Cookbook, *another book in this series on southern ingredients and foodways, Belinda Ellis taught biscuits all kinds of new tricks. Only an idiot would not ask her to come up with a bacon-enhanced biscuit to include in these pages. Her magic continues.*

MAKES 8 BISCUITS

---

8 ounces sliced smoky bacon
2 cups soft wheat self-rising flour
2 tablespoons firmly packed brown sugar
½ teaspoon freshly ground black pepper
4 tablespoons unsalted butter cut into ½-inch chunks,
　　placed in the freezer for 15 minutes
1 cup shredded sharp cheddar cheese, divided
¾ cup buttermilk, plus more if needed
1 tablespoon rendered bacon drippings

Preheat the oven to 425°. Line a baking sheet with parchment paper or use a Silpat.

In a heavy skillet over low heat, slowly cook the bacon until done. Drain on paper towels, reserving the rendered drippings. Finely chop the bacon and reserve.

Whisk together the flour, brown sugar, and pepper in a large mixing bowl. Cut in the butter until it is the size of small peas.

Stir the bacon and half the cheese into the flour mixture. Add the buttermilk and bacon drippings and stir to combine. If necessary, add additional buttermilk to create a sticky dough. Drop the biscuit dough by heaping tablespoons onto the baking sheet. Sprinkle the remaining cheese on top of the biscuits.

Place in the oven and bake for 12 minutes or until the biscuits are golden brown. Serve immediately.

Bacon, Egg, and Cheese Sandwich, New York City Deli Style

I know that as a southerner I'm supposed to want my bacon, egg, and cheese in a biscuit, but I have long been a fan of this perfect on-the-go breakfast sandwich found in New York City's delis and Korean markets. I think you may become a fan as well. While this variation is based on a broken-yolk fried egg, don't hesitate to scramble the egg if you desire. I like a slice of tomato and sometimes even onion on the sandwich. Wrap it up in aluminum foil or parchment paper and off you go to work or school.

SERVES 1

1 kaiser roll
1 tablespoon unsalted butter
2 large eggs
1 slice American cheese
3 slices cooked bacon, warmed
1 slice tomato (optional)

Slice the kaiser roll in half through its equator and toast.

Place a cast-iron or nonstick skillet over medium heat and add the butter. When the butter begins to foam, crack each egg into the skillet. As the whites of the eggs begin to set, use a fork and drag through the yolk, breaking it. Cook until the yolk is set, usually about 3 minutes.

Take the toasted kaiser roll and place the bacon on the bottom, then top with the eggs and then the cheese. Add the tomato if you wish and place the top of the kaiser roll over the sandwich. Serve immediately or do it deli style, wrapped in aluminum foil for portability.

Succulent Soups and Classic Salads

Many soups and salads wouldn't be the same without bacon; it can add depth, earthiness, smoke, and salt to any warm or cold dish. But most of all it always seems to add joy for the eater. And bacon fat is mystical stuff that can transform even a can of tomato soup into something great. What follows is a collection of recipes that join some of the best playmates with bacon. Some are classic, many down-home, but all are worth you taking them on a kitchen spin.

Chesapeake House Fish Stew

The Chesapeake House in Myrtle Beach, South Carolina, has been open for decades, and any local or regular visitor to the area will say it's on their list of favorites. Still family-owned, this restaurant has resisted the trend toward huge seafood buffets and continued its tradition of fresh, carefully prepared local seafood. The fish stew is very "low-country," meaning a bit spicy and tomato-based. Serve in a Crock-Pot for big parties. Any mild, flat, white fish will work. The smokier the bacon, the better.

SERVES 8–12

½ pound bacon, diced

1 cup chopped onion

5 cups water

3 pounds flounder filets

1 teaspoon Tabasco sauce

2 tablespoons Worcestershire sauce

1 tablespoon celery salt

Freshly ground black pepper, to taste

1 (8-ounce) can tomato paste

2 cups ketchup

Rice to make 8–12 servings

Fry the bacon in a medium skillet until crisp. Remove it from the pan and drain it on paper towels. Add the onions to the bacon drippings and cook until lightly brown. Reserve.

In a large soup pot, bring the water to a boil. Stir in the onions, drippings, bacon, fish, Tabasco, Worcestershire, celery salt, and pepper. Reduce heat to a simmer. Cook until the fish is done, about 10 minutes. The fish will begin to fall apart.

Stir in the tomato paste and ketchup. Simmer the stew for 2 hours or until thickened. Serve over rice.

For a more souplike result, cut the simmering time to 1 hour.

Almost the Pearl's Clam Chowder

When I was splitting my time between North Carolina and New York City, one of my favorite places to eat was the Pearl Oyster Bar in Manhattan. I never needed a menu. I knew what I wanted when I walked in the door: a lobster roll and their superior clam chowder. Owner-chef Rebecca Charles used her summers on the coast of Maine to create some wonderful eating experiences. I like her chowder because it isn't flour-laden and gloppy. She also uses bacon instead of salt pork. She uses double-smoked bacon, which you could certainly substitute in this recipe, but I find that applewood-smoked bacon seems to bring out the clam flavor. This is a great recipe for your DIY Basic Bacon (page 23).

SERVES 4

---

8 pounds fresh quahogs or cherrystone clams
¼ pound applewood-smoked bacon, diced
1 teaspoon cooking oil
1 large onion, chopped
2 large Yukon Gold potatoes, peeled and cut into ½-inch dice
1 cup clam juice, or reserved strained cooking liquid
3 cups heavy cream
Kosher salt and freshly ground black pepper, to taste
Chopped chives

Ideally, you should steam the clams yourself and not buy them in a can. To steam the clams, put them in a pot with a tight-fitting lid and a couple of cups of water. The process takes 3 to 5 minutes, depending on the size of the clam. As with any shell-fish, as soon as the shell is open, it's done. Reserve the broth for the chowder.

To make the chowder, in a 4- to 6-quart saucepot, render the bacon in the oil over medium heat. Add the onions and sauté until they are translucent, about 5 to 8 minutes. Add the pota-toes, stirring occasionally, and sauté for 3 minutes. Stir in the clam juice, reduce the heat to low, and simmer for 25 minutes. Stir in the cream and simmer for another 25 minutes, until the potatoes are tender. Add the clams and simmer for 5 more minutes. Season with salt and pepper.

Ladle the chowder into bowls and sprinkle with the chopped chives. Serve with oyster crackers.

Corn, Shrimp, and Bacon Chowder

Fresh summer corn is a thing of beauty, and it pairs incredibly well with some hints of bacon and seasonally caught shrimp. While this chowder has some thickness, it's not as thick as a Boston-style clam chowder, making it light and wonderful during the summer months. Please heed my directions on what I call milking the cob—scraping the cobs after you've cut off the kernels. There is such tremendous flavor in this residue of pulp and juice that it's a shame to let it go to waste.

SERVES 4

6 ears corn, husks and silks removed

4 slices bacon, cut crosswise into $\frac{1}{2}$-inch strips

8 green onions, both white and green parts, trimmed and thinly sliced

2 medium russet potatoes, peeled and cut into $\frac{1}{2}$-inch dice

2 tablespoons all-purpose flour

3 cups whole milk (you can also use low-fat milk, but the result will be a thinner soup)

1 teaspoon Chesapeake-style seafood seasoning

$\frac{1}{2}$ teaspoon dried thyme leaves

2 cups water

1 pound (30–40 count) peeled and deveined shrimp

Kosher salt and freshly ground black pepper

Place a dish towel on the counter. Cut the tip off of each cob of corn. Stand the corn vertically and use a sharp knife to slice off the kernels. Pour the kernels into a medium mixing bowl, then use the back of a knife and vigorously scrape the cobs over the bowl to get out all of the corn's "milk." The pulp and the liquid that comes from the cobs add a lot of flavor and will also help to thicken the chowder. Discard the cobs.

Place a 3-quart or larger saucepan over medium heat, add the bacon, and cook until the bacon is crisp, 6–8 minutes. Use a slotted spoon to transfer the bacon pieces to a plate lined with paper towels. Add the green onions to the saucepan, reserving some of the green for a later garnish. Add the potatoes and cook, stirring, until the green onions have gotten lazy, usually about 3 minutes. Sprinkle in the flour, and stir until it has dissolved into the bacon fat, about 2 minutes. While stirring, pour in the milk, seafood seasoning, thyme, and water.

Bring the soup to a boil, then reduce heat to a simmer and cook, stirring occasionally, for about 10–12 minutes or until the potatoes are tender when pierced with a knife.

Stir in the corn and shrimp and cook for about 3–5 minutes. Take care not to overcook the shrimp.

Taste for seasoning and add salt and pepper if needed. Stir in the reserved bacon pieces and the reserved green tops for garnish. Serve immediately.

White Bean and Bacon Soup with Bitter Greens

Bacon has long been a critical seasoning ingredient for southern cooks, and it really shines in this bone-warming soup. Dried white beans, which I grew up calling navy beans or great northerns, are also a reminder of our ancestors' dependence on beans during financially challenged times. While this soup is good anytime, it is especially comforting during the winter.

SERVES 6–8

---

1 (12-ounce) package applewood-smoked thick-cut bacon, roughly chopped

2 cups chopped yellow onion

2 tablespoons finely chopped shallots

1 garlic clove, finely minced

8 cups homemade or canned low-sodium chicken stock

1 pound dried white beans, soaked overnight, drained, and rinsed

6 sprigs thyme

¼ teaspoon hot pepper sauce (optional)

1 teaspoon kosher salt

Freshly ground black pepper

4 cups bitter greens, such as escarole, turnips, or collards, cut into thin strips

---

Toss the bacon into a 5-quart Dutch oven or large soup pot. Place it over medium heat and cook, stirring occasionally, until crisp, usually about 12 minutes. Remove the bacon with a slotted spoon and transfer to a paper-towel-lined plate. Add the onions and shallots to the pan and cook, stirring occasionally, until the onions are lazy and have taken on a bit of color, about 8–12 minutes. Throw in the garlic and cook for another minute.

Toss the reserved bacon back in the pan and pour in the stock, beans, thyme, hot pepper sauce (if using), salt, and a few grindings of pepper. Bring the soup to a boil, reduce heat to a simmer, and cover. Simmer for about 30 minutes, then uncover and cook until the beans are tender, about an additional 1½ hours. Make sure that the liquid is not evaporating too quickly.

When the beans are tender, stir in the bitter greens and cook for 2–5 minutes or until wilted. Ladle into soup bowls and serve immediately.

Classic Warm Spinach Salad with Tomatoes and Bacon Vinaigrette

From the moment I first ate a warm spinach salad with hot bacon vinaigrette, I was hooked—and I think most people are. If you've never attempted this, I think you'll be surprised at how utterly simple it is, and the results are show-stopping.

SERVES 4

6 slices bacon, cut crosswise into 1-inch pieces
1 medium onion, peeled, halved, and thinly sliced
2 cups chunks of heirloom tomatoes or grape tomatoes
⅓ cup champagne or other white wine vinegar
1 tablespoon sugar
1½ pounds (about 2–3 bunches) flat-leaf spinach, trimmed
    and cleaned, or 2 bags of prepared spinach leaves
Kosher salt and freshly ground black pepper, to taste

Place a large sauté pan over medium heat and add the bacon. Cook, stirring occasionally, until the bacon is crisp and browned, about 8–10 minutes. Using a slotted spoon, remove the bacon to a paper-towel-lined plate. Reserve 3 tablespoons of the bacon fat from the sauté pan and pour the rest in your bacon drippings jar.

Return the sauté pan to medium heat. Pour in the 3 tablespoons of reserved bacon fat and add the onions. Stir until just cooked and wilted, about 5–6 minutes. Add the tomatoes, vinegar, and sugar. Simmer this mixture until the liquid thickens slightly and the tomatoes are heated through, about 2–3 minutes.

Place the spinach in a large salad bowl and pour the hot tomato/onion mixture over the greens. Toss the spinach to coat with the dressing and slightly wilt the spinach. Season with salt and pepper and sprinkle the reserved bacon pieces over the top. Serve immediately.

NOTE ❊ Want to gild the lily with another southern favorite? Roasted pecans make a great "crouton" for this salad. It's simple to prepare them: Preheat the oven to 350°. Spread about ½ cup pecan halves on a rimmed baking sheet and place them in the oven until golden and fragrant, usually 10–15 minutes. Use them to top the spinach salad. Not necessary, but an excellent and tasty addition.

Frisée Salad with Poached Eggs, Lardons, and Shallot and Bacon Vinaigrette

This is a classic bistro-style salad and a recipe not to be missed. It is a favorite of the readers of my Weekend Gourmet column in Raleigh's News and Observer, *and I have published it in my magazine* Edible Piedmont *to great applause. This salad is beautiful to the eye and is one of my favorite taste experiences. The slow-moving, almost lavalike egg yolk coats the greens and helps to form a perfect collision of hot and cold, crisp and creamy, sweet yet tart—shucks, it hits each note of a perfect flavor profile and textural eating joy. If poaching an egg frightens you, don't hesitate to use a sunny-side-up or over-easy egg to complete this salad.* Lardons *is just a fancy French word for "strips of bacon."*

SERVES 6

½ pound thick-cut bacon
1 shallot, finely diced
3 sprigs fresh thyme
2 tablespoons Dijon mustard
6 tablespoons red wine vinegar
¼ cup extra-virgin olive oil
¼ cup water
Kosher salt and freshly ground black pepper, to taste
1 quart water
½ cup white wine vinegar
6 large eggs (farm stand preferred)
3 heads frisée, available at farmers' markets, Whole Foods
    Market, and other upscale grocers
1½ cups croutons

Cut the bacon into thick strips lengthwise, throw them into a cold skillet, and place it over medium-low heat. Cook slowly to render out all the fat. Remove the bacon with a slotted spoon and drain on a paper-towel-lined plate. Reserve the drippings for the vinaigrette.

Place the shallot, bacon fat, thyme, mustard, and red wine vinegar in the container of a blender, or a bowl if you're using an immersion blender. Purée all the ingredients until smooth, and while the blender is running, slowly add the oil and water. Season with salt and pepper and reserve at room temperature or refrigerate. The dressing will last for 3–4 days covered and chilled.

Pour the water into a wide 3-quart saucepan. Season the water with salt and white wine vinegar. Place over medium heat and bring to a simmer. I like to use a teacup to slide my eggs into the liquid. Carefully break one egg into a teacup and ease it into the water. Poach for about 5–6 minutes; the yolks should still be runny, but the white should be fully cooked. Remove the eggs from the water using a slotted spoon and set aside.

Wash the frisée and remove the center core stem. Mound the frisée equally on six salad plates. Sprinkle the greens with the bacon and croutons and drizzle with the bacon vinaigrette. Top each with a poached egg and serve.

Classic Iceberg Wedge with Bacon and Blue Cheese Dressing

A longtime steakhouse favorite, the iceberg wedge has come back into favor and is served in every type of restaurant in the country. There's a good reason—not many salads are this tasty. If you're not a blue cheese fan, you could use another aged cheese or even a ranch dressing instead. To gild the bacon lily, I suggest that you take an additional ¼ cup of crumbled cooked bacon and stir it into the dressing. Think about serving this salad with a beautifully grilled porterhouse steak or rack of lamb for an over-the-top experience.

SERVES 4

FOR THE DRESSING

1 cup sour cream

4 tablespoons good-quality mayonnaise

¼ cup finely chopped cooked bacon

2 tablespoons chopped fresh chives

1 tablespoon Worcestershire sauce

1 teaspoon dark steak sauce (like A-1)

2 garlic cloves, finely minced and worked to a paste

⅛ teaspoon ground cayenne pepper (optional)

1 tablespoon fresh lemon juice

1 cup (about 4 ounces) crumbled good-quality blue cheese

Kosher salt and freshly ground black pepper, to taste

1 head iceberg lettuce

$\frac{1}{2}$ cup crumbled cooked bacon

16 or so cherry tomatoes cut in half

4–6 ounces good-quality blue cheese, crumbled

$\frac{1}{4}$ cup chopped fresh chives

Freshly cracked black pepper, to taste

HOW TO CRACK WHOLE PEPPERCORNS EASILY

Cracked peppercorns give you intense flavor and another textural foil. To crack black pepper, pour out some peppercorns on a cutting board. Take your heaviest skillet and place it over the peppercorns. Lean into the middle of the skillet to slightly flatten the peppercorns so they don't roll off the cutting board. Using the edge of the skillet, press on the peppercorns until they crack.

To make the dressing, in a medium bowl combine all the ingredients except the salt and pepper, folding until well blended. Taste for seasoning and add salt and pepper as needed. Store in an airtight container, refrigerated, until ready to use.

To make the salad, cut the head of iceberg into quarters. Remove the root stem from each quarter, then place each on a salad plate. Sprinkle the bacon evenly over each serving. Divide the cherry tomatoes and the chunks of blue cheese among the plates.

If the blue cheese dressing is too thick for your taste, then thin it out with a little milk. Spoon 2 tablespoons or more of dressing on each serving and sprinkle the chopped chives on top. Give each serving a good sprinkling of cracked black pepper. This salad will hold up for about 30 minutes, so keep that in mind in your dinner planning.

NOTE ❋ This dip improves overnight and keeps nicely, refrigerated, for up to 2 weeks—although I doubt it will last that long before you eat it.

Baconized Burgers and Sandwiches

Think, for a moment, of a world without a BLT. Has there ever been a better use of white bread, mayonnaise, lettuce, and tomato than to surround it with bacon? I say not. What about smoky pork juices rolling around and commingling with ground meat seared to perfection? I can't imagine not having the opportunity to eat such creations. So take a ride through the recipes that follow to find the best ways to enjoy bacon between bread.

The BLT

The BLT is the second most popular sandwich, bowing only to the ham sandwich and not by many votes at all. It is the most democratic of any sandwich. People of all races, creeds, and purse sizes—and, yes, even politicos—can enjoy this humble meal. The ingredients are crucial to success; they should be first rate so all the flavors come through. The mayonnaise is key, because it brings all the flavors together. The bread must always be white and toasted.

SERVES 4

---

8 slices lightly toasted white bread (I like sourdough)
Great-quality mayonnaise (homemade is best, but
    southern styles like Duke's, JFG, Sauer's, or Blue Plate
    are acceptable)
4–8 (depending on size) 1/4-inch slices of a dead-ripe tomato
A minimum of 4 slices crisply cooked smoked bacon
    per sandwich
1 cup shredded lettuce (romaine is a good choice)
Kosher salt and freshly ground pepper, to taste
8 frilly toothpicks

Slather each slice of bread with as much mayonnaise as you like (I use about 1 tablespoon per slice). Divide the tomato slices among half of the slices of bread, then top with the bacon and about a 1/4 cup of shredded lettuce on each sandwich. Add salt and pepper; top each with a slice of bread remaining, mayonnaise side toward the bacon. Cut in half on the diagonal, insert a toothpick in each half, and serve.

NOTE ❋ A BAT—bacon, avocado, and tomato—is a nice change of pace from the original.

Fred's Fabulous Tuna Salad on Pumpernickel with Sprouts, Bacon, and Tomato

Everyone loves my tuna salad, which is really easy to make. My favorite version is topped with sprouts, bacon, and tomato (actually, I make the salad to make this sandwich). I think it will become a favorite of yours as well.

MAKES ABOUT 4 CUPS, FOR 6–8 SANDWICHES

6 (6-ounce) cans light chunk tuna packed in water
1 teaspoon garlic powder
1 teaspoon dried thyme leaves
½ cup sweet pickle relish
⅔ cup good-quality mayonnaise
1 tablespoon fresh lemon juice, depending on the
　　flavor of the mayonnaise
Salt and freshly ground black pepper, to taste
Sliced pumpernickel bread
Sprouts
2 slices tomato for each sandwich
At least 3 slices crisply cooked bacon for each sandwich

Drain the tuna well in a colander. Transfer to a mixing bowl and add the garlic powder, thyme, and pickle relish. Stir to combine.

Fold in the mayonnaise. Add the lemon juice if desired. Season with salt and pepper. Cover and refrigerate until chilled. Keeps refrigerated for 3 to 4 days.

For a sandwich, spread about ¼ cup or more on a slice of bread. Mound some sprouts atop the salad. Add 2 tomato slices. Tear 3 strips of bacon in half and arrange them on the tomatoes. Top the concoction with another slice of bread, cut in half, and enjoy.

The Fat Elvis

The South's favorite Tennessee rockabilly singer, Elvis, is said to have loved peanut butter, bananas, and bacon—all together, more often than not, and usually once a day. This recipe won't make you a star, but it will make you happy.

SERVES 1
(can be made in multiples for larger crowds)

---

2 tablespoons creamy peanut butter, or more to taste
2 slices Pepperidge Farm Sourdough Bread or similar
One banana, peeled and sliced into rounds
3 slices crisply cooked bacon
1 tablespoon unsalted butter

Spread the peanut butter over one side of each slice of bread. Add the banana and the bacon to one side and top with the other piece of bread. You could eat it just like this, but . . .

Melt the butter in a 10-inch skillet over medium heat. Add the sandwich and grill until golden, then turn it and cook the other side. Press down a bit on this side. When it's nice and toasty, remove it to a plate, slice it in half, and serve.

The 50/50 Burger

Heck, anyone can put bacon on top of a hamburger, but inside the burger? Absolutely. This style of bacon burger has become all the rage at many upscale restaurants around the country, and with some pretty upscale prices. Simply put, it's ground beef and ground bacon put together in a patty, and it is easy to do at home with a meat grinder or food processor. Slab bacon would be the best choice, but using bacon slices works great too. Just freeze the bacon before grinding. You've really got to try this burger for the perfect awesome blending of great flavors.

MAKES 8 HAMBURGERS

---

1 pound slab or sliced bacon
1 pound ground chuck (grass fed is wonderful)
Kosher salt and freshly ground black pepper
8 slices of your favorite cheese
8 hamburger buns, toasted
Mayonnaise; Bacon Fat Mayonnaise is awesome (page 17)
Mustard and ketchup as desired
Slices of tomato
Slices of sweet onion
8 fried eggs (optional but tasty)

If using slab bacon, keep it very cold before grinding. If using sliced bacon, freeze overnight.

Working quickly, cut the bacon into chunks that will fit through the meat grinder. Grind the bacon using the coarse die. If you're using the food processor, pulse the bacon until it resembles coarsely ground beef. Do this in small batches so as not to overheat the bacon with the friction of the machine.

Combine the bacon with the beef and form into 8 patties, not too thick. Refrigerate them on a sheet pan for 1 hour.

Preheat the gas grill or start a charcoal fire. When it's hot, remove the burgers from the refrigerator, season them with salt and pepper, and place them on the grill. Cook for about 8 minutes (and be prepared for flare-ups). Turn and cook another 4 minutes, add the cheese, and continue cooking another 4 minutes or until the burger is medium-well done or reaches an internal temperature of 165°. You cannot cook this burger less because of the bacon, but don't worry—it will be the juiciest burger you've ever had.

To build the burger, put your condiments on the bun, place a burger on the bottom, and add the tomato and onion slices and fried egg (get it?—bacon and eggs). Serve with plenty of napkins.

Green Chili and Bacon Cheeseburger

You cannot go to New Mexico without having a green chili cheeseburger. The best one is at Bobcat's Bite, just outside Santa Fe. This recipe is based on their burger. Of course you can't replicate the seasoning of their grill, but in the meantime, this burger is a darn good stand-in.

SERVES 6

2¼–2½ pounds freshly ground chuck
1 teaspoon kosher salt
1 teaspoon freshly ground black pepper
6 burger-size slices each American and Monterey Jack cheese,
    at room temperature
12 slices crisply cooked bacon
6 large sturdy hamburger buns toasted near the side of the grill
Mayonnaise
6 thick slices large red-ripe tomato
Crisp iceberg lettuce leaves
Slices of mild onion if desired
1½–2 cups roasted New Mexico green chilies, mild to hot,
    fresh or thawed frozen, chopped, warmed

Preheat the grill for high heat.

Mix the ground chuck, salt, and pepper together in a bowl. Gently form the mixture into six patties ½–¾ inches thick. Patties should hold together, but avoid handling them any longer than necessary. Arrange them on a platter or baking sheet to take to the grill.

Grill burgers uncovered over high heat, 1–1½ minutes per side. Move burgers to medium heat and rotate by a half turn for crisscross grill marks.

Cook 3½–4 minutes longer, turn once more, and cover each burger with cheese and top with bacon. Cook another 3½–4 minutes for medium doneness: a bare hint of pink at center of each crusty, richly browned burger. Remove from grill to a clean platter or baking sheet.

Lather the buns with mayo. Arrange tomato or any other optional topping(s) on each bun. Follow with cheese-covered burgers. Spoon the chilies over each. Crown with bun tops. Serve right away.

Grilled Chicken Breasts with Cheese and Bacon Jam

I promised you plenty of reasons to use bacon jam, and this is a good one. The somewhat neutral flavor palate of the chicken breasts provides a showcase for the seasoning and the cheese. The bacon jam kicks it up to new heights with its smoky sweetness.

SERVES 4

---

4 (6- to 8-ounce) boneless, skinless chicken breast halves

Kosher salt and freshly ground black pepper

1 teaspoon Italian seasoning

Vegetable oil spray

8 slices Italian fontina

8 slices good-quality sourdough bread

4 slices dead-ripe tomatoes, or more as needed

Slow Cooker Bacon Jam (page 36)

Mayonnaise, if desired

Season all of the chicken breasts with salt, pepper, and a sprinkling of the Italian seasoning. Spray lightly with the vegetable oil spray.

Preheat the grill or start the charcoal.

Place the chicken breasts on the grill and grill 5–8 minutes per side, depending on the thickness. You want the chicken breasts relatively firm to the touch and cooked through, but not dry. With about 2 minutes left before the chicken is done, place 2 slices of the cheese on each chicken breast. Close the lid and allow the cheese to melt. Add the bread to the grill and toast about 1 minute per side.

Remove the chicken and the bread to a platter and build your sandwiches. If you're using mayonnaise, spread the bread with it. Otherwise, cut each chicken breast on the bias lengthwise. Place each breast on the bread. Add tomatoes to each sandwich and top with a tablespoon of the bacon jam. Place the remaining slices of bread on the sandwiches, cut in half, and serve immediately.

Grilled Baconized
Pimento Cheese Sandwich

If you're trying to impress somebody or you're having a fancy cocktail party, then this is the pimento cheese to go with—and serving it as a grilled sandwich takes it over the top! Of course, the pimento cheese will be better if you use homemade mayonnaise, but I find that Duke's or JFG works without missing a beat. When I make this recipe I tend to use white cheddar cheese for visual appeal as well as taste.

MAKES ABOUT 1 PINT OR 8 HEARTY SANDWICHES

3 to 4 cups grated white sharp cheddar cheese

1 (4-ounce) jar whole pimentos, drained

Mayonnaise as needed

⅛ teaspoon onion powder

⅛ teaspoon ground red pepper

Dash or 2 of Worcestershire sauce

2 tablespoons sugar

6 slices (or more) crisply cooked bacon, chopped

16 slices of your favorite sandwich bread

Unsalted butter as needed to toast the sandwiches

If you have a food processor, this comes together quick and easy. Fit the food processor with a metal blade. Add the cheese and pimentos. Pulse several times to combine. Add about ½ cup of mayonnaise and pulse again. For a creamier pimento cheese, add some more mayo. Add the remaining ingredients and pulse until everything is well blended. Remove from the food processor to a bowl and stir in the bacon. Place it in an airtight container and refrigerate until ready to serve. Of course you can eat it now, but the flavors meld better when made a day in advance.

Line the bread up to make sandwiches. Slather as much pimento cheese as you want over half the slices. Top with the other slices of bread.

Melt the butter in a 12-inch skillet over medium heat. As the butter foams, add the sandwiches and cook for 2–3 minutes or until golden brown. Flip the sandwiches and cook another couple of minutes or until the second side is golden. Serve hot, with lots of napkins.

Dennis and Fred's Grilled Salmon BLT

More than a dozen years ago, I was working on a test shot with New York City food photographer Dennis Gottlieb. He wanted to do a marketing piece with a sandwich photograph. I came up with this idea, and after we got the sandwich on film, we ate heartily. Marinated tomatoes (even winter tomatoes taste good when done this way), lemony mayonnaise, good-quality thick-cut bacon, and grilled salmon add up to one extraordinary sandwich. It wasn't long after Dennis sent out his mailer that we both noticed salmon BLTs showing up on menus all around the city.

SERVES 4

---

4 plum tomatoes

1 teaspoon salt

1 teaspoon freshly ground black pepper

2 teaspoon balsamic vinegar

1 tablespoon chopped fresh basil or oregano

1½ cups good-quality mayonnaise

Juice of 2 lemons

Four 5- to 6-ounce salmon fillets, any pin bones removed

8 slices of your favorite bread (French works well)

4 pieces green leaf lettuce

8 slices smoked bacon, fried until crisp and drained on
    paper towels

Cut each tomato into 4–5 slices lengthwise. Place them in a bowl and sprinkle with the salt, pepper, and vinegar. Add the basil or oregano and toss to combine. Let stand at room temperature.

Combine the mayonnaise and lemon juice in a measuring cup.

Light a charcoal fire or preheat the gas grill to high. Oil the grill's cooking surface.

Place the salmon fillets skin side up on the grill and cook for about 5 minutes. Carefully turn them over and cook another 3 minutes for medium or to your desired degree of doneness. Transfer the fish to a platter.

Toast the bread, if desired, then spread the lemon mayonnaise on each piece. Place one lettuce leaf on 4 of the slices of bread. Place a salmon fillet on top of each lettuce leaf. Top with 2 slices of bacon. Equally divide the marinated tomatoes between the sandwiches. Top with the remaining bread. Cut in half and serve.

Bacon at the Center of the Plate

I know our first thoughts of bacon tend to lean toward breakfast, sandwiches, party foods, and burgers, but that's misleading us. Bacon brings out the awesomeness in many center-of-the-plate recipes. It's particularly good with seafood, and I've included several seafood-based recipes in this chapter. Lean cuts of meat benefit from bacon's inclusion. Pasta and bacon have been a longtime favorite combination, and bacon has also been used as a filler in meatloaf, stretching the ground meat and adding copious amounts of flavor. So here are some of my favorites that I hope will become yours too.

Bacon-Wrapped Quail with Pepper Jelly Glaze

My friend Hugh Lynn grew up in Texas hunting quail and shared this very easy recipe with me. He claims to have gotten it from an old hunting camp cook. Even without the wild quail, it's a tasty dish and an example of how bacon can enhance and protect the flavor of a lean bird.

SERVES 4
(2 quail per person)

---

8 quail, about 5½ ounces each, dressed
1 teaspoon kosher salt
1 teaspoon freshly ground black pepper
8 strips thick-cut bacon
½ cup green or hot pepper jelly, slightly melted
½ teaspoon Worcestershire sauce

Season each quail with ⅛ teaspoon of the salt and ⅛ teaspoon of the pepper. Wrap the bacon around the quail and secure it with a toothpick on butcher's twine.

Preheat the grill to medium-low.

In a bowl, whisk the pepper jelly and Worcestershire sauce until smooth.

Place the bacon-wrapped quail on the grill and cook, turning frequently, for 10 to 12 minutes, or until the bacon is beginning to caramelize in places and the quail have grill marks on all sides. Brush the quail with the glaze and continue turning, glazing, and cooking until birds are nicely glazed and grilled on all sides and the flesh is just cooked through, about 10 minutes longer.

Oyster Bacon Casserole

This casserole most definitely belongs in the center of the plate, but I would not think of having a Thanksgiving or Christmas meal without having oyster casserole as a side. So this is a double-duty recipe. You will notice that pepper is the only seasoning it gets, so pour the pepper on. I like using the whole-wheat crackers because they add a nuttiness that matches up with the bacon. Any leftovers can be gently reheated and then topped with some sunny-side-up eggs for a pretty special breakfast. And if a raw oyster just happens to get loose, well, chefs have to have a treat every now and again.

SERVES 10–12
(but can be cut in half; use an 8 × 8-inch dish)

---

1 quart plus 1 pint shucked oysters with liquor

1 (16-ounce) box whole-wheat Ritz crackers

1 pound bacon, diced and cooked crisp

2 sticks unsalted butter, melted, or more as needed

At least 1 tablespoon freshly ground black pepper

Preheat the oven to 350°.

Place the oysters in a colander with a bowl underneath to drain the liquor. Reserve the liquor.

Roughly crush the crackers, making sure you have some large pieces. In a 9 × 13-inch baking dish, sprinkle ⅓ of the crushed crackers on the bottom in an even layer. Layer about half the oysters and bacon over the crackers. Cover the oysters with another layer of crackers, and then layer the remaining oysters and bacon. The final layer will be the remaining crackers over the top of the oysters.

Mix the butter together with the reserved oyster liquor to equal 1½ cups. Pour the mixture evenly over the casserole. Sprinkle the casserole with copious amounts of black pepper. You want to literally be able to see the black pepper.

Bake for 15–20 minutes or until the casserole is a little brown but still moist. Serve hot.

Seared Scallops with Bacon

Every time I visit Virginia Beach, Virginia, I visit Welton's Seafood Market on Laskin Road. He always seems to get his hands on the most perfect dry-packed sea scallops I've ever found in a store. When you start with perfection you don't need to do much to them, but this little twist on the standard seared scallop is heavenly. Be sure to buy only dry-packed large sea scallops; the cheaper wet-packed ones just won't sear. The caramelization that happens in the searing process brings out the natural sugars in the scallops and is a huge part of their flavor profile.

SERVES 4

---

6 slices applewood-smoked thick-cut bacon,
    cut into ¾-inch pieces like a lardon
16 (about 1 pound) large dry-packed sea scallops
Kosher salt and freshly ground black pepper
2 tablespoons minced shallot
1 cup dry white wine
2–3 tablespoons unsalted butter

Add the bacon pieces to a large sauté pan and place over medium-low heat. Cook the bacon slowly, stirring occasionally until brown and crisp, usually 8–10 minutes. Remove the bacon with a slotted spoon and place on a paper-towel-lined plate to drain.

Pour off the excess fat into your bacon drippings jar, leaving a thin coat in the bottom of the pan. Increase the heat to medium. Slice each scallop through the equator, forming two rounds. Add the scallops to the pan, sprinkle lightly with salt and pepper, and cook for about 2 minutes. You should get some nice browning occurring. Turn the scallops and cook an additional 2 minutes. Do not overcook the scallops. They should feel like the tip of your nose when you touch them.

Remove the scallops from the pan and place in a serving dish. Toss the shallots into the pan and cook until they are wilted, usually a couple of minutes. Add the white wine and scrape up any brown bits from the bottom of the pan. When the wine has reduced by about half, usually about 4 minutes, remove from the heat and swirl in the butter. Pour the butter mixture over the scallops, top with the reserved bacon, and serve immediately.

Rockfish Enrobed in Bacon

The jewel of the Chesapeake Bay, rockfish—or, as it's known to many folks, wild striped bass—is such a good eating fish. It's meaty, nicely firm, and not fishy. Here we take rockfish filets, wrap them with bacon, and serve with a little citrus sherry vinaigrette to create a company-worthy entrée that's easy enough to make during the week.

SERVES 4

4 (6- to 8-ounce) rockfish filets (thick end preferred)
Kosher salt and freshly ground black pepper
12 strips applewood- or hickory-smoked bacon
2 teaspoons Dijon mustard
2 teaspoons honey
1 tablespoon sherry vinegar
1 red grapefruit cut into supremes (segments),
    plus juice squeezed from the remaining membrane
1/4 cup fruity extra-virgin olive oil

Season the filets with salt and pepper. On a cutting board, lay slices of bacon so that they overlap slightly. Place one filet on each set of bacon slices. Wrap the filets tightly with the bacon. Set aside.

Whisk together the mustard, honey, vinegar, and grapefruit juice. Sprinkle in some salt and pepper. Slowly whisk in the oil. You could also do this in a blender if desired.

Take a large nonstick sauté pan and place it over medium-high heat. When the pan is hot, place the fish in the pan seam-side down. Cook until the bacon has become a deep golden color on all sides, about 9 minutes total. You will need to turn the fish several times to get the bacon cooking evenly.

Remove the fish to a platter. Toss the grapefruit sections over and drizzle with the dressing. Serve immediately.

Stuffed Pork Chops with Smoked Gouda and Bacon

This is a pork-on-pork dish. The mild flavor inherent in pork chops combines with the pronounced flavor of the smoked Gouda and bacon for a tummy-filling and satisfying supper. You really want to use a bone-in pork chop, because it helps with the stability of the stuffing. And while you could bake or broil these, there's no better way to cook them than on the grill.

SERVES 4

1 cup (about 4 ounces) shredded smoked Gouda cheese

8 slices bacon, cooked and crumbled

1/3 cup chopped fresh flat-leaf parsley

1/8 teaspoon freshly ground black pepper

4 at least 2-inch-thick center-cut bone-in pork chops

Olive oil for drizzling

Kosher salt and freshly ground black pepper

Preheat the grill for medium heat.

Toss the cheese, bacon, parsley, and ⅛ teaspoon of the black pepper into a medium bowl. Use your hands to combine.

Lay a pork chop on a cutting board and with a sharp knife (a boning knife is a good tool here) held parallel to the board, cut a pocket in the chop all the way to the bone. Make sure you leave the sides intact. Repeat with the remaining chops and then stuff as much of the cheese mixture as you can into each pocket. You can close the pocket with a toothpick or (my preference) tie the chop with a little butcher's twine. Drizzle each chop on both sides with oil and season with salt and pepper.

Lightly oil the grill grate. Place the chops on the grill and cook for about 5 minutes. Rotate each chop 45 degrees and cook an additional 3 minutes. Turn and continue cooking until the pork is done and has reached an internal temperature of 145°. Do not overcook the pork.

Transfer to a serving platter and serve immediately.

Beef Filets Wrapped with Bacon and Sage

Filet mignons are among the most popular steaks in the country, but I think they need a little bit of help in the flavor department. That's where the bacon and the sage come in. Sage is commonly used to flavor beef in Argentina, and I think it adds a lot of interest to the steak. The method here is for the grill, but what follows the recipe is a note on how to do this in a cast-iron skillet. We are also going to blanch the bacon slightly, so that it will cook and crisp up faster, allowing the filets to be cooked to a rare to medium-rare state.

SERVES 4

---

4 strips thick-cut smoked bacon
4 (1½-inch-thick) filet mignons
16 fresh sage leaves
Kosher salt and freshly ground black pepper

Place the strips of bacon in a saucepan and cover with cold water. Bring to a simmer over medium heat and cook for about 6–7 minutes. Drain the bacon and pat very dry. Set aside.

Pat the steaks as dry as you possibly can. Take each strip of bacon and place 4 sage leaves along it. Wrap the bacon/sage slice around the equator of each steak and then tie with kitchen twine. Liberally season with salt and pepper and set at room temperature while you get the grill ready.

Start a charcoal fire or preheat a gas grill. When the fire is ready or the grill is hot, place the filets on the grill. Cook the steaks for about 2 minutes, then rotate them a quarter turn and cook for another 2 minutes. Turn the steaks and repeat the process on this side. You're cooking the steaks for a total of about 8–10 minutes for medium-rare; pressing the steak should feel like pressing on the tip of your nose. The bacon also should be well charred at this point.

Transfer the steaks to a platter and let them sit for about 5 minutes. Cut the strings and serve.

NOTE ❋ To cook in a cast-iron skillet, place over high heat until the skillet begins to smoke. Place the steaks in the skillet and cook for about 2 minutes. Rotate the steaks a quarter turn and cook for 2 minutes more. Flip the steaks and cook for an additional 3–4 minutes on the second side. Again transfer the steaks to a platter and let stand for about 5 minutes.

Mama's Bacon-Wrapped Meatloaf with Fred's Brown Sugar–Chili Glaze

Meatloaf was a favorite at our house growing up. Mama always wrapped her meatloaf in bacon and then poured Bennett's Chili Sauce over the top. Bennett's is slightly different than other brands because it includes a little pickle. I've tweaked her recipe by adding some ground veal and making a more pronounced glaze. She thought it was better than hers, which from her is very high praise.

SERVES 6–8

¼ cup chili sauce (I like Bennett's Brand, and so did Mama)

2 tablespoons firmly packed light brown sugar

2 teaspoons cider vinegar

2 teaspoons vegetable oil

1 medium onion, chopped

2 garlic cloves, minced

2 large eggs

1 teaspoon dried thyme

1 teaspoon salt

½ teaspoon freshly ground black pepper

2 teaspoons yellow mustard

2 teaspoons Worcestershire sauce

¼ teaspoon hot red pepper sauce

½ cup milk or buttermilk

2 pounds meatloaf mix (1 part ground chuck, 1 part ground veal, 1 part ground pork)

⅔ cup crushed saltine crackers (about 16) or ⅔ cup oatmeal or bread crumbs

⅓ cup minced parsley

6 ounces thin-sliced bacon (about 8 slices)

Mix the chili sauce, brown sugar, and vinegar in a small bowl; set aside.

Preheat the oven to 350°. Heat the oil in a medium skillet. Add the onions and garlic and sauté until softened, about 5 minutes; set aside to cool.

Mix the eggs with the thyme, salt, pepper, mustard, Worcestershire, pepper sauce, and milk or buttermilk. Add the egg mixture to the meat in a large bowl, along with the crackers (or oatmeal or bread crumbs), parsley, onions, and garlic; mix the meat mixture with a fork until it's evenly blended and does not stick to the bowl. (If the mixture does stick, add additional milk or buttermilk, a couple tablespoons at a time, and continue stirring until it stops sticking.) Turn the meat mixture onto a work surface. With wet hands, pat mixture into a loaf approximately 9 by 5 inches.

Cover a wire rack with foil; prick foil in several places with a fork. Place the rack on a shallow roasting pan lined with foil.

Set formed loaf on rack. Brush the loaf with all of the chili sauce glaze, then arrange the bacon slices crosswise over the loaf, overlapping them slightly and tucking them under to prevent curling.

Bake the loaf until the bacon is crisp and the loaf registers 160°, about 1 hour. Cool for at least 20 minutes. Slice and serve.

Southern Carbonara with Linguine

Carbonara is a traditional Italian sauce usually made with pancetta, egg, and cheese. You certainly can take this recipe and add diced pancetta, but I think you will be surprised by how good this sauce is when you use a nice lightly smoked bacon. Linguine is the classic noodle, but this will also work with angel-hair, spaghetti, or even penne.

SERVES 4

---

8 slices bacon, cut into ¼-inch pieces
1 pound linguine
3 large eggs (farm stand preferred)
¾ cup grated Asiago cheese, plus more for serving
½ cup half-and-half (low-fat works)
½ cup cooked baby green peas, or thawed peas if frozen
 (optional)
Kosher salt and freshly ground black pepper

In a large skillet or sauté pan, cook the bacon over medium heat, stirring occasionally until crisp, about 8–12 minutes. Using a slotted spoon, transfer it to a paper-towel-lined plate.

Set a large pot of water over high heat and bring to a boil. Salt the boiling water generously. As Mario Batali says, "It should taste of the sea." Add the pasta and cook until al dente.

While the pasta is cooking, in a large bowl whisk together the eggs, cheese, and half-and-half. Hold at room temperature. Drain the pasta, leaving as much water clinging to it as possible. You need to work quickly here. Add the hot pasta to the egg mixture. Throw in the reserved bacon and the peas, if using. Toss vigorously to combine. The heat from the pasta will cook the eggs. Season with a little salt and pepper and serve immediately with additional cheese if desired.

Grilled Pizza with Bacon Jam and Prosciutto

The great pizza emporiums of New York City and the Northeast feature pizza with a thin, crispy, slightly blackened crust. Once you've had it, you will likely come to crave it. You'll also notice that the really great pizza joints use old wood- or coal-fired ovens. Bet you can make that happen on your grill. The pizza dough recipe is designed to give you a thin crust. A couple of tricks I've learned: put the cheese down first, then the sauce, and don't put more than four ingredients on the pizza, so it will slide off the peel easily (we're not as skilled as the pizza pros). Also, the cornmeal is critical for success. It acts as a sort of ball bearing to help the pizza off the peel. Even if you don't make the dough, the topping is great on ready-to-bake pizza rounds or flatbreads.

MAKES 4 PIZZAS

1 cup warm (105–110°) water

1 teaspoon sugar

1 teaspoon active dry yeast

3 cups all-purpose flour

1 teaspoon kosher salt

1 teaspoon olive oil

1 pound fresh mozzarella, sliced, or fresh ricotta

Slow Cooker Bacon Jam (page 36)

Caramelized onions

Baby spinach

6 slices prosciutto, torn into small pieces

Additional flour as needed

Cornmeal for dusting

Pour the water into a measuring cup, add the sugar, and sprinkle the yeast over the water. Let sit until frothy, usually about 5–10 minutes.

Add the flour and salt to the bowl of an electric mixer fitted with a dough hook. Add the yeast mixture and mix on low speed until the dough is combined. Pour in the olive oil and continue to mix on low. When all the ingredients are blended, knead the dough on medium speed for about 5 minutes or until the dough is smooth and elastic.

Dust the work surface lightly with flour and form the dough into a ball. Spray a bowl with vegetable spray and place the dough in the bowl. Cover with plastic wrap and let sit in a warm place until doubled in size, usually about 1½ hours.

Turn the dough out onto a floured surface and knead 4 or 5 times. Form the dough into a ball and cut into 4 equal parts. Shape each into a disc and dust with flour.

Light a fire in the grill. After about 10 minutes, place a ceramic baking stone on the grill grate and close the lid. Then open the upper and lower dampers all the way. Let the temperature get close to 500°.

Using a rolling pin, roll each disc into a 10- to 12-inch circle. Lightly dust a pizza peel with cornmeal, then top with the dough. Throw some cheese over the dough, then smear on some bacon jam and add the onions, spinach, and prosciutto.

Dust the pizza stone with cornmeal. Carefully slide the dough off the peel onto the preheated baking stone. Cook for about 10 minutes or until the dough is crisp and the cheese is melted. Remove to a cutting board and cut into serving slices. Repeat with the additional discs.

Side Dishes
Spiced with Bacon

One of the greatest and most prevalent uses of bacon in the South is for seasoning. This chapter explores that phenomenon with old southern classics, classics with a twist, and a few new adventures.

Grandmother's Stewed Green Beans with Bacon

Southerners would just call these "green beans" or "snap beans" because this is the way that every southern grandmother cooked her green beans. You really are "stewing" the beans, and you may never cook green beans any other way after tasting these. You can also make these beans in a Crock-Pot or pressure cooker.

SERVES 8

6 slices bacon, thinly sliced crosswise
1 cup chopped onion (about 1 medium)
2½ pounds green beans (stem ends removed),
    cut into 1-inch lengths
1 (32-ounce) box reduced-sodium chicken broth,
    or homemade stock
Kosher salt and freshly ground black pepper

Place a 5-quart Dutch oven or heavy pot over medium heat, add the bacon, and cook until browned, 10 to 12 minutes.

Add the onions to the pot and cook for 5 minutes

Pour the green beans and broth into the pot. Season lightly with salt and pepper. Bring to a boil; reduce heat to a low simmer, and cook until green beans are very tender, about 1–1½ hours. Taste and reseason with salt and pepper. I like lots of pepper.

Creamy Grits with Bacon and Sage

This unique take on grits is the perfect accompaniment for many of winter's heartier dishes. I love this with pork chops and pork roast or as a base over which to ladle beef stew. You can cut back on the milk, but the grits will be less creamy. If you're using farm-stand or heritage grits, cover the grits the night before with water and then drain before cooking. This will shorten the cooking time.

SERVES 4

4 slices thick-cut applewood-smoked bacon, chopped

1 teaspoon chopped fresh sage leaves

4 cups milk

¾ cup grits

3 tablespoons unsalted butter, or more to taste

½ teaspoon kosher salt, or more to taste

⅛ teaspoon freshly ground black pepper, or more to taste

Place a 3-quart saucepan over low heat. Add the bacon and cook for about 8–10 minutes or until crisp and browned. Use a slotted spoon to remove the bacon from the saucepan and transfer to a paper-towel-lined plate. Reserve. Throw the chopped sage into the saucepan and cook in the bacon fat until the sage is very fragrant, usually less than a minute. Stir in the milk and bring to a boil.

In a steady stream, pour in the grits, whisking constantly until smooth and creamy. Keep at a low simmer until the grits are tender, which could be anywhere from 10 minutes to 30 minutes, depending on which grits you're using. Stir in the butter and taste for seasoning. Add additional salt and pepper if needed.

Pour into a serving bowl and top with the reserved bacon. Serve immediately.

NOTE ❋ You can also stir in some goat cheese or Swiss cheese if desired. Cheddar doesn't quite work with the sage.

Brussels Sprouts with Pancetta and Balsamic

If you had asked me a few years ago what my favorite Brussels sprouts recipe would be, I would have laughed and told you there is no such thing as a good Brussels sprouts recipe. This one changed my mind. Now I can't wait for Brussels sprouts to come into season and will eat this dish almost once a week through late fall, winter, and early spring. This recipe is adapted from a local Italian restaurant that served it as a special appetizer for the winter; the dish has grown so popular they can't take it off the menu.

SERVES 4–6

1 pound trimmed Brussels sprouts
Water
4 ounces diced pancetta
2 tablespoons olive oil
3 garlic cloves, minced
Kosher salt and freshly ground black pepper
2 tablespoons balsamic vinegar

Fill a 3-quart saucepan about half full of water. Place over high heat and bring to a boil. Add the Brussels sprouts and cook 4–5 minutes. Drain and run under cold water for a couple of minutes. Spread a few layers of paper towels on the counter and spread the Brussels sprouts over the paper towels to dry.

Place the pancetta in a cold cast-iron or heavy-bottomed sauté pan. I use a carbon steel skillet for this. Cook over medium-low heat until the pancetta is crisp and has rendered its fat. Remove the bacon and reserve the fat.

Add the olive oil to the fat. When the oil is warm, add the sprouts and garlic. Pan-roast until the sprouts begin to caramelize, turning a few times, so that all sides of the sprouts are browning, about 15 minutes. When the sprouts are tender, add the reserved pancetta. Season with a generous pinch of salt and freshly ground black pepper. Remove from the heat and toss with the vinegar. Place in a serving dish. Serve hot.

Bacon-Barbecued Baked Beans

Every family needs at least three great baked bean recipes to get them through potlucks, dinner on the grounds, family reunions, and of course tailgating. This recipe comes by way of one of my cousins and is her favorite go-to bean recipe. I like the inclusion of the apple, and you can change it up every time just by changing the barbecue sauce you use. It works well with fried chicken and is an awesome side for Texas-style barbecue.

SERVES 10–12

8 slices bacon, cut in half crosswise
1 medium onion, diced
1 medium green pepper, diced
$\frac{3}{4}$ cup your favorite barbecue sauce
$\frac{1}{4}$ cup light firmly packed brown sugar
$\frac{1}{4}$ cup apple cider vinegar
2 tablespoons Dijon mustard
$\frac{1}{4}$ teaspoon freshly ground black pepper
1 Granny Smith apple, diced
1 (15-ounce) can pork and beans
2 (15-ounce) cans pinto beans, drained

Preheat the oven to 325°.

Place the bacon in a large sauté pan. Put the pan over low heat and slowly cook the bacon until it is only partially cooked, flipping once, about 4 minutes per side. Remove the bacon from pan and drain on paper towels, reserving about 1½ tablespoons of bacon drippings and adding the rest to your bacon fat container. Add the onions and peppers to the bacon drippings in the pan and sauté until tender, about 5–6 minutes.

Meanwhile, mix the barbecue sauce, brown sugar, vinegar, mustard, and pepper. Add the beans and the sauce mixture to the sautéing veggies and bring the pan to a simmer.

Pour the beans into a greased 13 × 9-inch casserole dish or ovenproof pan. Top with torn bacon pieces, then bake until beans and sauce have cooked down and thickened substantially, about 80–90 minutes. Let stand to slightly thicken and serve while nice and warm.

Mama's Field Peas, Almost

Whether I was visiting my grandmother, at a family reunion, or coming home, somebody always cooked a pot of field peas for me. My grandmother used to tell me I was going to turn into a field pea because I ate so many. This is the way my mama cooked them, with an addition of fresh herbs from me. They are just earthy and delicious and doggone good.

SERVES 4–6

---

2 slices thick-cut smoked bacon, chopped
½ cup diced onion (about 1 small)
4 cups field peas such as Dixie Lee's
3 cups homemade or canned low-sodium chicken broth
4 sprigs thyme, tied together with butcher's twine
2 bay leaves
Kosher salt and freshly ground black pepper, to taste

In a 3-quart saucepan, add the chopped bacon, spreading it evenly in the bottom of the pan. Place it over medium-low heat and slowly render the bacon. This usually takes about 5–10 minutes. Using a slotted spoon, remove the crisp bacon and place it on a paper towel to drain.

Increase the heat to medium and toss in the onions. Cook, stirring occasionally, until the onions are translucent, about 2–3 minutes. Add the peas, broth, thyme, and bay leaves.

Bring to a boil over medium-high heat. Reduce heat to a simmer and cook for 25 minutes. Taste the peas for doneness. Many times pink eyes are tender yet retain their shape at 25 minutes. However, don't be surprised if it takes 35 minutes for them to be completely done.

Remove from the heat. Fish out the thyme and bay leaves and discard. Season with salt and pepper and serve immediately or at room temperature.

Low-Country Red Rice

I love Charleston and its low-country ways. Red rice is one of the delights of the region, and there are nearly as many ways to prepare red rice as there are cooks in Charleston. But the basic recipe remains the same: rice, tomatoes, and bacon fat simmered together to make something delicious! This dish is perfect served with fried seafood; just about every good fried seafood shack in the area uses it as a side dish. Don't stop there, though; try it with cooked greens and country sausage. This recipe is based loosely on the red rice served by See Wee restaurant, just north of Mt. Pleasant, South Carolina.

SERVES 8

4 strips bacon, cut into 1-inch pieces
2 onions, finely chopped
1 (6-ounce) can tomato paste
2¼ cups water
3 teaspoons kosher salt
2–3 teaspoons sugar
½ teaspoon freshly ground black pepper
1 cup long-grain rice
8 tablespoons bacon grease (optional)

Place the bacon in a large sauté pan and place over low heat. Fry the bacon until it's crisp and most of the fat has rendered, about 10–15 minutes. Remove from the pan and drain on paper towels.

Sauté the onions in the bacon drippings left in the pan. Add the tomato paste, water, salt, sugar, and pepper. Bring the mixture to boil, then add the rice and extra bacon grease (if desired).

Bring to boil again, stir well, and then reduce heat to low and cover. Do not open and stir again until rice is completely cooked (follow the directions on the rice package); stir in crumbled bacon and serve.

Yes You Can—Smoked Macaroni and Cheese with Bacon

I'm really tempting fate by monkeying around with my family and neighbors' all-time-favorite mac and cheese recipe. Why not add a little smoked cheese and bacon to a classic? The result? On tasting, all my Doubting Thomases raved over the additions. Thanks to Linda Johnson, my back-door neighbor, for a great starting recipe for me to fool around with.

SERVES 4–6

Butter to grease the casserole dish
Water
1 pound elbow macaroni
9 tablespoons unsalted butter, divided
1 cup (about 4 ounces) shredded Muenster cheese
1 cup (about 4 ounces) shredded mild cheddar cheese
1 cup (about 4 ounces) shredded sharp cheddar cheese
1 cup (about 4 ounces) shredded Monterey Jack cheese
2 cups half-and-half
1 cup (8 ounces) cubed Velveeta
4 ounces smoked farmer's cheese or other smoked
     Brie-like cheese
2 large eggs, lightly beaten
8 slices smoked bacon (try the DIY Basic Bacon, page 23),
     chopped and cooked until almost done
1/4 teaspoon seasoned salt
Freshly ground black pepper
Any wood chunk

Preheat the smoker or grill to 350°.

Butter a 2½-quart deep casserole dish.

Fill a large pot, 4 quarts or larger, about half full of water. Place over high heat and bring to a boil. Add the macaroni and cook until the pasta is just tender, usually about 7 minutes. Do not overcook, as it will cook further in the oven. Drain the pasta and return it to the pot.

Melt 8 tablespoons of the butter and stir it into the macaroni. In a large bowl blend the shredded cheeses together. Pour the half-and-half into the pot with the macaroni and add 2 cups of the shredded cheese, the Velveeta, all of the farmer's cheese, the eggs, and the bacon. Sprinkle in the seasoned salt and 5–6 grindings of pepper. Stir all the ingredients to combine. Pour into the prepared casserole and sprinkle with the remaining cheese and dot with the remaining butter.

Smoke until it's bubbling around the edges and just slightly browned on top, about 1 hour. Serve hot.

A Few Sweet Treats and a Beverage

Some might see this chapter as silly, because we all know that bacon is not destined to be included in absolutely everything (only *most* everything). But these recipes reflect how good bacon can be with sweets if you use a little common sense and good basics. Even some of the failures were good; experimenting is half the fun in writing a cookbook. These are the best, and my many tasters agreed. They were just disappointed they had to wait for the book to come out to have them again.

Oatmeal Chocolate Chip Cookies with Bacon

For me, an oatmeal cookie with chocolate chips is a chocolate chip cookie. Magpie's, a local Knoxville, Tennessee, bakery, puts Benton's bacon, from just up the road in Madisonville, Tennessee, in a chocolate chip cookie, so I thought, Why not add a smoky bacon to my favorite oatmeal chocolate chip cookie recipe? Love 'em.

MAKES ABOUT 60 COOKIES

1¾ cup all-purpose flour
1 teaspoon baking soda
½ teaspoon salt
½ cup unsalted butter, softened
3 tablespoons chilled bacon fat
¾ cup firmly packed light brown sugar
½ cup sugar
2 large eggs, lightly beaten
3 cups old-fashioned oats
2 cups semisweet chocolate chips
1 cup cooked and finely crumbled bacon

Preheat the oven to 375°. Line a cookie sheet with parchment paper or coat with nonstick cooking spray.

Whisk together the flour, baking soda, and salt.

In a large mixing bowl combine the butter and bacon fat. Beat in both sugars until light, about 2 minutes. Add the eggs one at a time, beating well after each addition. With the mixer on low speed, add the flour mixture and oats. Then add the chocolate chips and bacon.

Scoop using a 1-tablespoon cookie scoop or tablespoon and drop onto the prepared pan. Bake for 8–10 minutes, or until lightly browned. Cool for 2 minutes on the baking sheet and then place on a cooling rack. Store in an airtight container.

Tennessee Bacon–Marshmallow Pie Cookies à la MoonPies

I wanted Belinda Ellis, a Tennessee native and a wonderful pie maker, to try making a MoonPie with bacon. That's a challenge. Belinda went to work to create a dessert that is great when fresh from the factory, but even better when homemade and with bacon.

MAKES 18 SANDWICHES

1½ cup all-purpose flour

1 cup whole-wheat pastry flour

¼ teaspoon baking soda

½ teaspoon salt

¼ cup chilled vegetable shortening or bacon drippings

¼ cup chilled bacon drippings

1 cup sugar

1 large egg

½ cup sour cream

1 teaspoon vanilla extract

1 (7-ounce) container marshmallow fluff

16 ounces semisweet chocolate, chopped in small pieces

9 slices bacon cut in half and cooked crisp (optional)

Preheat the oven to 350°. Line a cookie sheet with parchment paper or coat with nonstick cooking spray.

Whisk together both flours, the baking soda, and the salt. Beat the shortening and bacon drippings until combined. Gradually add the sugar and beat for 2 minutes. Add the egg and beat until blended. Alternately add the flour mixture and the sour cream until blended. Stir in the vanilla extract. Remove the dough from the bowl and wrap tightly with plastic wrap. Refrigerate for 1 hour.

Scoop by heaping tablespoons or use a cookie scoop to shape the dough into balls about 1 inch in size. Drop the dough balls about 2 inches apart on the prepared pan. Use shortening or bacon drippings to grease the bottom of a drinking glass. Press each dough ball to about ¼ inch thick.

Bake for 10 minutes or until set. The cookies will not brown. Cool 5 minutes on pan and then move to a rack to cool completely.

Working with one cookie at a time, scoop 1 tablespoon of marshmallow fluff onto the bottom of half of the cookies. If you want, put ½ tablespoon of the marshmallow fluff on the cookie, place a piece of bacon in the center, and top with the other ½ tablespoon of fluff. Press another cookie on the top to make a sandwich. Refrigerate the cookies for at least 1 hour.

Melt the chocolate over a double boiler. Dip each cookie. Sprinkle chopped bacon over the top. Refrigerate until set.

Salted Caramel Bacon Brownies

Salted caramel and bacon, two of the trendiest foods of the moment, paired with everybody's favorite, an ooey-gooey brownie. You'll get the vapors!!

MAKES 16 BROWNIES

FOR THE FILLING

½ cup sugar

3 tablespoons bacon drippings (or, if you prefer
    less bacon flavor, use just 1½ tablespoons plus
    1½ tablespoons unsalted butter)

¼ cup heavy cream

FOR THE BROWNIES

1¼ cup sugar

¾ cup cocoa powder

½ teaspoon salt

½ cup unsalted butter

1 teaspoon vanilla extract

2 large eggs

⅓ cup all-purpose flour

6–8 slices pig candy (page 40), cut in ½- to 1-inch pieces

Preheat the oven to 325°. Line an 8- or 9-inch square baking pan with foil. Coat the foil with butter.

To make the caramel filling, heat the sugar in a medium saucepan with a heavy bottom, stirring constantly. The sugar will lump and then melt to a deep golden brown. Watch carefully—sugar burns easily. Add the bacon drippings and the butter, if using, and stir vigorously. Remove from the heat and drizzle in the cream carefully (it will steam and bubble), beating rapidly to mix. When the mixture is smooth and the bubbling has calmed, set it aside to cool for at least 15 minutes.

To make the brownies, combine the sugar, cocoa powder, and salt in a mixing bowl. Melt the butter, pour it over the mixture, and stir until well blended. Add the vanilla and eggs, and stir. Then stir in the flour just until blended; the batter will be very thick

Spread half of the brownie batter in the pan. Top with all but 1 tablespoon of the caramel and spread evenly over the brownie layer. Use a spoon to drop the remaining brownie batter gently onto the caramel. Use an offset spatula or the back of a spoon to gently spread the batter over the caramel.

Bake for 30–35 minutes or until a toothpick inserted is almost clean when removed. Remove from oven. Drizzle the reserved caramel over the brownies. Place the pig candy gently on top of the brownies and return the pan to the oven for 3–5 minutes to set.

Cool in the pan for 10 minutes. Lift the foil from the pan and place on a cooling rack to cool completely. Cut into small squares.

Fred's Take on Bacon Ice Cream
with All the Goodies

It's amazing how much the salty goodness of bacon can add to a dessert that we've loved since childhood. The juxtaposition of the textural ingredients against the creamy egg-rich goodness of the base makes for one of the best ice creams you'll ever eat.

SERVES 6–8

4 cups heavy cream

1¼ cups firmly packed dark brown sugar

4 egg yolks

1 teaspoon sea salt

½ cup finely chopped crisply cooked bacon

⅓ cup semisweet chocolate chips

¼ cup toasted chopped pecans

¼ cup Grade B maple syrup

Combine the cream and sugar in a heavy 3-quart saucepan and place over medium-high heat until it's hot and the sugar is completely dissolved, stirring occasionally. Do not bring to a boil.

In a small bowl, beat the egg yolks until smooth. Slowly whisk in 1 cup of the cream and sugar mixture. Pour the egg yolk mixture back into the saucepan, whisking constantly. Cook over medium heat, stirring continuously, until the mixture coats the back of a wooden spoon, about 6–8 minutes. Do not bring to a boil.

Pour the mixture into a container and refrigerate overnight or up to 2 days.

Pour the chilled mixture into an ice cream freezer and continue according to the manufacturer's directions. When the ice cream is almost done, usually about 15 minutes into the freezing process, add the bacon, chocolate, pecans, and maple syrup. Continue until the ice cream is the consistency of soft serve. Pack it into a container and keep it in the freezer overnight.

Remove the ice cream before serving to let it soften slightly. Try not to eat all of it in one sitting.

Bacon-Infused Bourbon

I wasn't going to do this. Bourbon is good just like it is. And yet it's tempting to jump into the trendiness of it. So what the heck, here it is: homemade bacon bourbon. No need to pay the big bucks at your local watering hole.

MAKES ABOUT A FIFTH OF INFUSED BOURBON

8 slices thick-cut bacon
1 750 ml bottle bourbon (not the great stuff, please)

Place the bacon in a cold heavy skillet. Put the skillet over medium-low heat and slowly cook the bacon to render the fat. Keep careful watch so that you don't burn it. If necessary, lower the heat. This process takes about 10–15 minutes. Remove the bacon and set aside for another use.

Pour the bacon drippings through a strainer into a measuring cup. Make sure you have at least ¼–⅓ cup of bacon drippings. If you don't, then cook some more bacon.

Combine the bacon drippings and the bourbon in a jar with a tight-fitting lid (a quart Mason jar works well). Let the mixture stand at room temperature for 24 hours. Occasionally pick up the jar and swirl the contents.

Place the jar in the freezer for 1 hour to allow the fat to solidify. Remove from the freezer and then, using a spoon, remove the solidified fat and discard.

Line a strainer with a coffee filter or six layers of cheesecloth. Strain the bourbon, then place it in a clean bottle and store it in the refrigerator for up to 2 months. Use in your favorite bourbon recipe or drink straight with a couple of ice cubes.

Acknowledgments

I'm honored to be part of UNC Press's Savor the South series, and really happy to represent bacon.

This is a book of influences—from everyday cooks, chefs, cure masters, and other food writers. Every one of them has a love for bacon and usually a story to go with it. As you read through the book, you'll meet many of them in the recipe headnotes. I love listening to people talk about food. The stories they tell are always tales of history, family, and love.

Let me salute my assistant, Kyle Wilkerson, for his hard work with me on this tome. At one point I thought we had "cured" his hands as we tested and retested the DIY Bacon recipes. He was wise council during this project, and I appreciate all he did. I'm not the best of bakers, but thankfully my close friend and fellow author in the series Belinda Ellis is, and she worked with me on most of the baking recipes. Be sure to check out her book *Biscuits*.

Elaine Maisner brought this project to me and has, as usual, been a great support with a keen eye for improvement. This is our second book together, and, well, she's just a great editor. There are other folks at UNC Press who deserve mention too: Alison Shay, Mary Caviness, Gina Mahalek, Matthew Somoroff, Kim Bryant—thank you all.

I would not be an author without the support of Toni Allegra, Joan and Don Fry, Pam Hoenig, the late John Edgerton, and Kat Thompson. Thanks as always.

And to Laura and Carter, my true north: love you both.

Index